# LUTHERAN QUARTERLY BOOKS

## Editor

Paul Rorem, Princeton Theological Seminary

## Associate Editors

Timothy J. Wengert, The Lutheran Theological Seminary at Philadelphia and Steven Paulson, Luther Seminary, St. Paul

*Lutheran Quarterly Books* will advance the same aims as *Lutheran Quarterly* itself, aims repeated by Theodore G. Tappert when he was editor fifty years ago and renewed by Oliver K. Olson when he revived the publication in 1987. The original four aims continue to grace the front matter and to guide the contents of every issue, and can now also indicate the goals of *Lutheran Quarterly Books:* "to provide a forum (1) for the discussion of Christian faith and life on the basis of the Lutheran confession; (2) for the application of the principles of the Lutheran church to the changing problems of religion and society; (3) for the fostering of world Lutheranism; and (4) for the promotion of understanding between Lutherans and other Christians."

For further information, see www.lutheranquarterly.com.

The symbol and motto of *Lutheran Quarterly,* VDMA for *Verbum Domini Manet in Aeternum* (1 Peter 1:25), was adopted as a motto by Luther's sovereign, Frederick the Wise, and his successors. The original "Protestant" princes walking out of the imperial Diet of Speyer 1529, unruly peasants following Thomas Muentzer, and from 1531 to 1547 the coins, medals, flags, and guns of the Smalcaldic League all bore the most famous Reformation slogan, the first Evangelical confession: the Word of the Lord remains forever.

*Living by Faith: Justification and Sanctification* by Oswald Bayer (2003).

*Harvesting Martin Luther's Reflections on Theology, Ethics, and the Church,* essays from *Lutheran Quarterly* edited by Timothy J. Wengert, with foreword by David C. Steinmetz (2004).

*A More Radical Gospel: Essays on Eschatology, Authority, Atonement, and Ecumenism* by Gerhard O. Forde, edited by Mark Mattes and Steven Paulson (2004).

*The Role of Justification in Contemporary Theology,* by Mark C. Mattes (2004).

*The Captivation of the Will: Luther vs. Erasmus on Freedom and Bondage,* by Gerhard O. Forde (2005).

# THE CAPTIVATION OF THE WILL

*Luther vs. Erasmus on Freedom and Bondage*

Gerhard O. Forde

*With an Introduction by*

James A. Nestingen

*Edited by Steven Paulson*

WILLIAM B. EERDMANS PUBLISHING COMPANY
GRAND RAPIDS, MICHIGAN / CAMBRIDGE, U.K.

Wm. B. Eerdmans Publishing Co.
255 Jefferson Ave. S.E., Grand Rapids, Michigan 49503 /
P.O. Box 163, Cambridge CB3 9PU U.K.

Printed in the United States of America

09  08  07  06  05  04      7  6  5  4  3  2  1

**Library of Congress Cataloging-in-Publication Data**

Forde, Gerhard O.
The captivation of the will: Luther vs. Erasmus on freedom and bondage /
Gerhard O. Forde; edited by Steven Paulson.
p.      cm. — (Lutheran quarterly books)
Includes bibliographical references.
ISBN 0-8028-2906-6 (pbk.)
1. Luther, Martin, 1483-1546. De servo arbitrio. 2. Free will and determinism —
History — 16th century. 3. Erasmus, Desiderius, d. 1536. De libero arbitrio diatribe.
4. Free will and determinism — Religious aspects — Christianity —
History of doctrines — 16th century.
I. Paulson, Steven D.   II. Title.   III. Series.

BJ1460.L85F67   2005

233'.7'0922 — dc22

2005040508

www.eerdmans.com

To Donald Juel,

colleague and friend,

*in memoriam*

# Contents

*Foreword*, by Steven Paulson     ix

*Preface*     xvi

Introduction: Luther and Erasmus on the Bondage
of the Will, *by James A. Nestingen*     1

1. The Argument about Scripture     23

2. The Argument about God     31

3. The Argument about Our Willing     47

4. The Argument about Christ and Salvation     61

Postscript     77

Sermons

    *The Easy Yoke*     83

    *Justification by Faith Alone*     86

    *A Word from Without*     91

    *On Getting Out of the Way for Jesus*     94

    *The Perilous Journey*     99

    *Go Away, Jesus!*     102

# CONTENTS

*I Chose You* 105

*On Death to Self* 108

*We Are Being Transformed* 112

*What Matters* 116

# Foreword

Luther finished his best book, by his own account, with a remarkable personal address to Erasmus. Although it was assuredly not tongue-in-cheek, it was nevertheless a double-edged sword if ever there was one. He told Erasmus, "You and you alone have seen the hinge on which everything turns, and have gone for the jugular."[1] There was something purgative, clarifying, and ultimately fruitful when Luther finally got an opponent worthy of himself, someone who quit dealing with trifles like the papacy, purgatory, or indulgences. Instead, Erasmus sought to kill what Luther called "our cause" by making it a mere reformation of the church. When Luther referred to "our cause," however, he was not speaking in the singular about himself alone, nor was he speaking in the plural merely about the faculty at Wittenberg or even the growing numbers of pastors, monks, and citizens who began taking up the preaching of the gospel. When Luther said "our cause," he was referring to the work of the triune God, no less, and specifically the cause of the Holy Spirit to make life where there is only death. Luther was convinced by Scripture and reason that the Holy Spirit worked by means of preachers who proclaimed salvation in Christ apart from the law by faith alone.

---

1. Martin Luther, *The Bondage of the Will,* trans. J. I. Packer and O. R. Johnson (Grand Rapids: Fleming H. Revell, 1957), p. 319; author's translation. Subsequent citations in this foreword will be given parenthetically in the text.

This meant that early on in Luther's best book Erasmus simply became irrelevant — except as a honing wheel for Luther's own sharp theological sword. Erasmus became merely the occasion for a volcanic explosion by a theologian who had, by most other accounts, already written his best works.

The historical introduction by James Nestingen provides the background needed at this point for the circumstances around the debate and its aftermath. Nevertheless, by his own admission, Luther entered more than a debate with another theologian when he finally took up his pen to respond to Erasmus' *Diatribe*. Luther felt he was put again under the harsh schooling of the Holy Spirit who calls forth preachers of the law and gospel by cooking and roasting them over a spit. Erasmus was left behind while God worked with a greater theologian, and Luther was not ashamed to say it: "By your studies you [Erasmus] have rendered me also some service, and I confess myself much indebted to you. . . . But God has not yet willed nor granted that you should be equal to the subject of our present debate. Please do not think that any arrogance lies behind my words" (320). Small theologians shudder at this kind of statement from Luther. Who is he but another voice with another opinion? Especially in relation to the learned Erasmus! Yet while he wrote this book, Luther himself began to refine the argument that is, after all, no less than "the Reformation." It became a book not about free will as a human faculty but about Jesus Christ and the Holy Spirit who in relation with the Father are relentlessly going about justifying the ungodly.

Luther then realized what this meant for the church and its unity. Discord and schism can be ended in the church only by keeping the entire focus of theology on this central matter of the proclamation of Christ for faith alone. This is important for both those who wish to see Luther as a reformer leading a movement within the catholic church and those who see him as one more heretic and self-appointed prophet breaking the concord of the church with his bellicose rhetoric. Sedition, schism, and heresy were well underway before Luther, and were represented by both the papal party and also the new spiritual prophets popping up around Luther and claiming his teaching as their own. For that reason, Luther offered sincere praise of Erasmus along with a biting declaration of what really marks the difference between schism and unity in the church: "If those who have attacked me in the past had done as you have done, and if those who now boast of new spirits and revelations would do the same also, we should have less sedition and sects and more peace and concord. But thus it is that God, through Satan, has punished our unthankfulness" (319). Luther had endured years of inadequate attacks that only demonstrated the real source of discord. The proper attack upon him and his theology was necessary so that the true confession could be elicited for what makes the unity of the church: "if we believe that Christ redeemed us by His blood, we are forced to confess that all we are was lost; otherwise, we make Christ either wholly superfluous, or else the redeemer of our least valuable part only; which is blasphemy and sacrilege" (318). Gerhard Forde calls this move "taking the argument to another level." He has understood where theology's jugular vein is, just as Luther appreciated Erasmus for having exposed it so clearly even though it should also have been Erasmus' own lifeblood.

There are not many who have been willing to follow Luther as he is "forced to confess" the captivation of the will. There are even fewer who will confess with him just who Jesus Christ is and what he is doing with sinners. Just so, there are not many who have been willing to embrace what this implies for preaching. Yet what a vast difference it makes for a preacher to stand before a congregation and assume their wills are bound rather than to stand before a group and assume their wills are merely in need of motivation. The difference is as great as that between God's work through the Holy Spirit and through Satan. Then again, how many have been willing to say what Luther says about having a God who is preached or a God who is not preached? For that reason Luther's *Bondage of the Will* operates as a kind of litmus test for what one is going to become theologically. The heirs of Erasmus are many, of Luther few, and identification with churches called "Lutheran" has not had much effect on the difference. Gerhard Forde has used his teaching office to witness the vast difference between a theology that operates by inference from the law and a theology that leads to what Luther calls "categorical" preaching. In short, that means that whatever communication does not give Christ to sinners unconditionally is error that leads to death. The free will is demonstrably not Jesus Christ. So Luther concluded his summary of Scripture in his book this way: "that whatever is not Christ is not the way, but error, not truth, but untruth, not life, but death, [and so] it follows of necessity that 'free-will,' inasmuch as it neither is Christ nor is in Christ, is fast bound in error, and untruth, and death" (307). This kind of logic allows for no imaginary middle ground, gray area, or synthesis of works. There is what Luther calls a division at this point that brooks no mending or alteration. At Christ the free will meets its end, and yet precisely there is the beginning of true faith. Who has dared to say this much as a preacher or theologian?

It is with great appreciation and anticipation, then, that I introduce this book that joins the seasoned work of Luther with that of a teacher like Professor Forde. Many of us have grown to respect him over the years for his honesty and directness about the most vital matter of how to preach Christ to the people who need him. It is for that reason that Professor Forde was gracious enough to include here a set of sermons preached mostly at the chapel at Luther Seminary over the course of his teaching. His own previous work entitled *Theology is for Proclamation* attests to the same concern found in this book on the captivation of the will. If Luther's argument is correct, then it opens the way to better preaching. As Professor Forde exposes some of the layers of argument in Luther's *Bondage of the Will,* he leads directly to how one preaches, and so into his own sermons. It is hard to forget such sermons as "Go Away, Jesus!" and "The Perilous Journey." They help teach the art of distinguishing law and gospel in such a way that we discern what God is doing to save sinners, and how to declare it, despite the prevalence of Erasmian theology inside and outside the church.

As is true from the earliest of Gerhard Forde's books, the chief concern is to learn the place of the law and its limit. Since Erasmus could not discern the limit of divine law, all that he thought and said must be inferred from that very law, including the power of the will to fulfill it (at least in some small way). This in turn leads back to the old pious wish to be found righteous in one's self rather than receiving righteousness outside one's self in Christ alone. As Luther expressed it directly to Erasmus, "In order to keep 'free-will' standing, you must invoke a *synechdoche,* to wrest all that is said in the Scriptures against ungodly men and limit it to man's brutal part only, so that his rational and truly human part may be preserved" (309). The part implies the whole. The law implies a power to fulfill it. "Ought" implies "can." All of these are the kind of operating assumptions that have been the very stuff of "modern" theology, and skeptical philosophy for that matter. When the limit is not drawn properly between law and gospel — that is, drawn eschatologically — the limit must be placed elsewhere, such as between one's higher reason or will and one's lower animal body. Professor Forde has also routinely pointed out why this seems to most theologians preferable to Luther's simple theo-logic. It means discontinuity for the self. That means death before resurrection, even for the theologian.

Luther lays out what Forde often calls "the eschatological limit" in a very interesting way in his book. Near the end of the book Luther speaks about "three lights": nature, grace, and glory. The great question of nature is what most theologians today call "theodicy," that is, why the good suffer and the bad prosper. The answer to this question always seems to be a perceived injustice on God's part. Preaching, or the light of grace, teaches us to trust God, who at great cost has redeemed us while yet ungodly and so is "for us" in the very form of his unconditional promise. But then we seem unsatisfied with this as well and start fearing election — how is it that God "crowns the ungodly freely, without merit, and does not crown, but damns another, who is perhaps less, and certainly not more, ungodly" (317). This is, as Forde has often shown, a version of the problem of election or predestination. And so we flop from one fear to another. Once again, God seems the only one to blame for this kind of lawless unrighteousness. Consequently, there are not many who have been willing to say what Luther says next. As the light of *grace* solved the question of nature by giving you a promise to live by, so the light of *glory* will solve the problem of election "when the light of the Word and faith shall cease, and the real facts, and the Majesty of God, shall be revealed as they are" (316). Forde has been able to say this, which means he speaks of faith alone as the way God justifies a sinner — only because it looks forward to the day when there will be *no more faith!* The Word alone saves, but only until its "light" shall cease — that is when we will see Christ plainly and directly. The church itself comes to an end! Faith ends. Preaching ends. Most theologians, and so also preachers, have not been willing to come to an end before the majesty of the Lord. But that means they have ended up substituting other things for the real proclamation.

I take both Luther's book and Professor Forde's book that you hold in your hands as the same kind of call to preach in such a way that faith alone results because there is no other option — that is, unless you count blasphemy as an option, and blasphemy is only another way of saying "no option." Their mutual call to the church is to preach that God is just. He was, is, and will be just. Specifically, God is just in reconciling the world to himself through Jesus Christ by ending the old and creating anew. So Luther finally calls Erasmus out on the carpet for a good chastisement, but here includes himself: "To think that we cannot for a little while *believe* that He is just, when He has actually promised us that when He reveals His glory we shall all clearly *see* that He both was and is just!" (315). Such is what it means to hear God's own preacher give us the Word in such a way that we wait in tense hope to *see* what we hold already in the hiddenness of *faith* itself. While it is true that even a printed sermon is not a preacher for you, it is taking another step toward a theology for proclamation. So you may take this combination of historical background, a theological essay on Luther's *Bondage of the Will,* and the collection of sermons that follow as what Professor Forde would call the pause between yesterday's preaching and tomorrow's.

As a taste of what is to come, I offer Luther's own conclusion to his argument. He rather bluntly ended the book by saying to Erasmus, "you failed." He was equally blunt about the reason for Erasmus' failure: "you are ignorant of Christ," he said (320). Luther then offered an assertion, and even a prayer, not on the basis of his own authority but on the basis of Christ's: "not all will go astray if you or I go astray. God is One Who is proclaimed as wonderful among His saints, so that we may regard as saints persons that are very far from sanctity" (320). Such a conclusion nicely fits Forde's combination of preaching and teaching in this book. He has always taught and preached so that we may regard as saints persons who are very far from sanctity. Jesus Christ is just in justifying those far from sanctity as the Holy Spirit makes faith where and when it pleases him. No argument is more exciting theologically than this one, as it goes right for the jugular. So, enjoy both Martin Luther and Gerhard Forde doing theology as it should be done.

STEVEN PAULSON
*Luther Seminary*

# *Preface*

Writing a book on Luther's *Bondage of the Will* is a foolhardy business — not because the arguments are so hard to understand but rather because they are difficult for sinners to take. The arguments are so massive that it is difficult to encompass them in the written text. Furthermore, they propose virtually — as the Greek has it — a *metabasis eis allo genos,* a raising of the issues to a higher plane.

But how can this "raising" come about? After years of teaching and seeking to understand some of the basic arguments, I have thought that it might be useful to isolate and analyze some of these main arguments. Consequently, this book takes the shape of an analysis of four basic arguments, each contributing to the sense of the whole.

Limiting the analysis to four arguments has both advantages and disadvantages, of course. It has the effect of narrowing the scope of the text. Thus the reader may find several topics inadequately treated or even neglected altogether. But it is hoped that in the course of the reading itself, the point of the method will emerge. The contention of this book, as I have already proposed, is that in Luther's reply to Erasmus we shall find quite a different way of doing theology, a raising of the issues to a higher level. This is not easy to explain; we can get at it through analysis and argument about the text itself.

Added to the whole difficulty is the nature of the argument itself. Erasmus, it should be recalled, insisted that even if true, the bondage of will and all that goes with it should not be laid before the eyes of the ignorant masses, lest they get the wrong idea and escape their moralistic prison! The result has been as Luther predicted. The people, and now even the professors, know practically nothing of this doctrine — knowledge of which Luther considered absolutely essential to salvation! Small wonder that the church of Martin Luther's vision has lost much of its drive for that salvation. It has lost its object (God) and spends its time on itself and its own supposed freedom. At any rate, the purpose of this book is to further a recovery by the church of its own rightful object and purpose.

Nothing would be more salutary in the life of the church today than a careful reading of Luther's *Bondage of the Will*. This book intends to provide at least the beginning for such reading.

A few remarks are necessary for reading this text. The quotations are taken either from the translation of *The Bondage of the Will* by J. I. Packer and O. R. Johnston entitled *Martin Luther on the Bondage of the Will: A New Translation of* De Servo Arbitrio (Grand Rapids: Fleming H. Revell, a division of Baker Book House Company, 1957), hereafter "Packer," or from the Rupp translation in *Luther's Works,* vol. 33, ed. Ulrich S. Leupold and Helmut T. Lehmann (Philadelphia: Fortress, 1965), hereafter "LW 33." In either case, page references are included in the citations.

My title, *The Captivation of the Will,* was chosen to indicate something of the dynamic of Luther's treatise and the God with whom Luther is dealing. *The Bondage of the Will* should not be seen primarily as a negative work or merely one more theological debate, but as a desperate call to get the gospel preached. It is intended to be a summons, not a dirge. It is the attraction of the argument that is all important. It is full of humor and theological gusto!

Finally, this book is not, strictly speaking, what scholars might like to call scholarship. Erasmus is the representative of that kind of scholarly enterprise in this exchange with Luther — but only the representative. Maybe the world does not need that anymore when it comes to Luther's real concern. I have no intention here of questioning that scholarly enterprise in its proper place nor am I entering into contention with it in this book. What is needed is treatment of the debate that will make clear the real discussion and what is at stake. So, I have another purpose here than adding another monograph to Luther studies. For that reason there are no long, protracted arguments with other scholars. This work is really a search for Luther's mind and heart. And, of course, his will! What I am looking for is the "logic," or better, the "theo-logic," of Luther's radically other view of bondage.

# Luther and Erasmus on the Bondage of the Will

## JAMES A. NESTINGEN

Of all Luther's opponents, only two left any lasting legacy. One was Thomas Cardinal Cajetan, dispatched by the papacy to meet with the troublesome monk early in what became the Reformation. Brilliant, refined, and learned, Cajetan was a classic insider, both politically and theologically. He had the papal connections to commend him for such a meeting and a command of the theology of St. Thomas that still stands out in the history of Thomism.

Erasmus, Luther's second worthy, was an equally classic outsider. He, too, could count on his connections. A master of networking, he had won chairs at the tables of the powerful throughout Mediterranean Europe and into the North as well, with special connections in England. Though he grew up speaking Dutch, he was above all a linguist, fully at home in Latin and fluent in Greek. His scholarship had gained him honors throughout the academic world. But for all of this, Erasmus was an itinerant, moving from faculty to faculty, though mostly in the Upper Rhine Valley between Strasbourg and Basel, and a loner.

Theologically, too, Erasmus followed his own course. Shaped by the simple piety of the Brethren of the Common Life who had raised him and then by Renaissance humanism, he was skeptical of, if not hostile to, the Thomistic tradition of official medieval Catholicism. He was much more interested in manners and morals, seeking in Scripture and other ancient literature the ideal patterns of personal and public life. His impatience with metaphysical abstractions was also a factor in his growing apprehensions about Luther.

Connections and forebodings combined in Erasmus' dramatic attack on Luther, the *Diatribe* of 1524. The older humanist had given the young reformer critical support in the earlier years of the Reformation, to the point where it was commonly observed that Erasmus had laid the egg which Luther hatched. Friends in power pressured Erasmus accordingly, urging him not only to disassociate himself from the reformer but to state a public challenge. For this purpose, Erasmus chose an issue that he considered peripheral theologically, one in which he assumed there ought to be some room for differences of opinion. That way, he could give Luther's ears a public boxing without doing any real damage to the coalition moving reform.

Whatever Erasmus' intention, the *Diatribe* shook Luther and his Wittenberg colleagues like a tremor. Erasmus had both standing and position. An excommunicant and officially an outlaw, Luther had nothing comparable. Widely known and celebrated though he might be, he was still a minor academic from a fairly new faculty in a small town in an obscure part of eastern Germany. And in addition to the difference of standing, Luther had other insistent pressures making their demands, including the signs of a developing war that materialized in the Peasants' Revolt of 1525. From his perspective, the timing of Erasmus' challenge could hardly have been worse.

Together, the factors at play were enough to stall a reply. But finally Luther went to work on an answer to Erasmus, producing one of his most important works, *De Servo Arbitrio* or *The Bondage of the Will*. Because Luther's arguments are so closely tied to Erasmus' attack, it is important to set them in their historical context. The theological framework of the argument should also be surveyed. Against this background, Gerhard Forde's theological use of Luther's arguments can then be introduced.

## The Context of the Debate

The debate between Luther and Erasmus erupted at a critical point in the middle 1520s, just as the combinations of forces set loose by the Reformation were threatening to shatter the unity of the church and the peace of the Holy Roman Empire, which included Germany and its environs. Europe appeared to be coming apart.

Earlier in the 1520s, the powerful but loosely associated coalition that had driven the Lutheran reform movement had already begun to show some signs of stress. Charismatic in the sense that it had gathered around Luther as a profoundly appealing figure, the movement had already survived numerous attempts by the papacy and the empire to stop it. But the ties that bound the forces gathered around Luther were loosening, and the potential for disaster increased concomitantly.

Luther had his own interpretation of what drove the movement behind him. He was an academic who also served as a parish priest, and so he characteristically understood the developments of the reform's earlier years in biblical terms. As he had studied the Psalms and the New Testament, particularly Paul's letters to the Romans and the Galatians, he had been pushed in his own mind to a different way of reading Scripture. His hermeneutic, shaped in a crucible formed by the biblical text and intense personal struggle, focused on the cross of Christ and heightened anticipation of God acting to shape a new future for creature and creation. Luther himself described his way of interpretation as a "theology of the cross" as opposed to a "theology of glory." Later scholars have associated his heated expectation with the apocalypticism of the apostle Paul and the prophet Isaiah.

Working this way, Luther began with God's act in the crucifixion and resurrection of Christ Jesus instead of the long tradition of domesticating grace into a process of moral reform that begins with human initiative and response. The God who creates out of nothing and raises the dead does not depend on levels of personal appropriation to balance the divine effort. Rather, Luther put it this way in the form of a thesis: "the love of God does not find but creates that which is pleasing to it."

3

The triune God is even now at work, through the preached word and the administered sacraments, to do just that.

Beginning here, the Reformation was for Luther first, foremost, and always a matter of witness. Official papal and political efforts to repress him and the reform, with accompanying theological controversies, drove him to other, correlated conclusions. By 1520, he had challenged the argument that the papal office defines the authenticity and fidelity of the church; he argued further that the German laity as represented by its political leadership had the authority to proceed with reform and defined faith in terms of the freedom of the gospel. Proceeding in the same way, Luther would continue through the Reformation to draw out other correlations and distinctions. But whether early or late, for him all of this was consequential of the original premise at the center of everything: God's justifying restoration of creature and creation in Christ Jesus.

For this reason, Luther's original goal was not so much reform of the church, a problem in which he developed a secondary interest, as it was the reform of preaching. Working from the biblical sources, he was convinced that the church had betrayed its heritage. A reformation worthy of the name was above all a matter of restoration of the biblical message, with the theology of the church being retooled accordingly. Justification *sola fide,* by faith alone, was the central argument of the reform as he conceived it. But the doctrine was not an end in itself, as though restoration of proper definitions would suffice. As he understood it, the doctrine of justification claims the center because it shapes the faithful teaching through which God creates and sustains faith — that is, the gospel.

Other forces in the coalition that made up the Lutheran reform movement had different agendas. They included the humanists, politicians involved in a growing German nationalism, and other groups with social and economic complaints.

The party that gave Luther his strongest early support, another loose confederation of like-minded scholars, developed out of the school of what has been termed Renaissance humanism. This movement originally emerged in Mediterranean Europe in the later fourteenth and fifteenth centuries. It included some of the most important literary, political, and artistic figures of the time: Dante, Boccaccio, Petrarch, Machiavelli, Leonardo da Vinci, and Michelangelo. By Luther's time, the movement had taken root in Northern Europe in the universities and associated communities. Though there were some great artists involved — Lucas Cranach and Albrecht Dürer stand out — the northern European Renaissance was primarily literary, working through extensive correspondence. Erasmus was the key figure in this network.

Southern or northern, the humanists shared several convictions. The most basic was the belief that the ancient world — particularly Rome, Athens, and Jerusalem — had access to the original wellsprings of human culture and that the intervening centuries had been a time of decline and loss. It was a deeply romantic movement in this sense, energized by the conviction that there was a time in which things were ultimately right in the human community and that the original sources would reveal the patterns that had made it so. For this reason, humanist scholars immersed themselves in the ancient languages of the Mediterranean, Greek and Latin, to gain access to the sources. Erasmus' motto, *ad fontes,* to the sources, held for them all.

But it was not scholarship for its own sake. Seeking the ancient patterns and principles defining culture, the humanists shared a further conviction that once obtained, their findings could be used to reverse the decline and restore both personal and public life. They were generally skeptical of abstractions if not downright contemptuous and impatient with what they regarded as speculative schemes. Armed with their knowledge of the ancients, the humanists wanted to begin with what is immediately available to human knowledge and experience.

Finally, the combination of these two convictions produced in humanism a practical orientation to reform. The humanists cultivated what would now be termed a proper lifestyle, with a pragmatic concern for the workings of everyday life. With this, the humanists were generally moralists, seeking ways to motivate proper behavior. As usual, the personal and public earnestness showed a darker underside: a rejection of those philistines who did not share these concerns. Among the northern humanists, this attitude commonly took the form of cutting satires like Erasmus' own *In Praise of Folly* or Ulrich von Hutten's *Letters of Obscure Men.*

Luther was trained in the methods and assumptions of Renaissance humanism in his earlier studies. In addition to knowing Latin, the European language of education and commerce at the time, he was well at home in Greek. He also had a working knowledge of Hebrew based on the studies of a great German humanist, Johannes Reuchlin. Luther's passionate pursuit of the biblical text had some roots in humanism. He also knew other ancient literature extensively, enjoying particularly Aesop's Fables and the work of Cicero. It was enough to make the German humanists consider Luther an ally and assume that his early protests and theirs were sprung from a common source.

One of the great treatises of 1520, Luther's *To the German Nobility,* indicates his awareness of the second party instrumental among those supporting reform. The nobility he addressed ranged from minor property holders and mayors of small cities to sovereigns of fairly large territories, like Frederick the Wise, the elector of Saxony. Like members of the American House of Representatives, the nobility were keenly aware of both their own authority and the limits of that authority. They were not generally noted for their piety. For all the moralism of the humanists, gatherings of those who held the offices of the Holy Roman Empire — the diets which met at cities like Worms, Speyer, or Augsburg — drew prostitutes from all over Germany. The night before the Diet of Worms, the bishop of Augsburg nearly lost his shirt gambling over cards.

Although church and state were bound together in overlapping layers and responsibility, a couple of factors inclined the nobility to defy the church's injunctions and support Luther. One was German nationalism. Mediterranean Europe, those Romance-language nations located south of a line stretching roughly from the Adriatic into the southern part of the Netherlands, generally disdained the Germanic-language Europeans north of the linguistic line. The Italians cultivated this disdain as an art, all the while exploiting northern resources — at least according to the Germans, whose resentment died hard. Another source

6

of sympathy for the Lutheran protest arose out of attempts by the church to wield power in the world. The papacy and related officials had consistently meddled in the German nobility's affairs. There were many politicians, including Luther's sovereign, Frederick, who were eager to throw off the church's hegemony and take religious matters into their own hands.

So when Luther appealed to Germany's politicians, he already had significant sympathy. This support, particularly Frederick's, had proved decisive in staving off the papacy's repeated efforts — one of them, Cardinal Cajetan's mission — to quell the disturbance that began with the indulgence protest. For whatever they believed in matters of faith, the German nobility had other pressing political concerns at stake in the reform and worked accordingly.

Late in 1520 Pope Leo excommunicated Luther when he was unable to undercut Luther's political support. Charles V, who had been elected Holy Roman Emperor over Leo's objections, still saw a potential disaster in the developing reform and so called the Diet of Worms in the spring of 1521 to settle the matter. Unable to dislodge Luther's support, Charles did succeed in putting the nascent Lutheran movement under the ban. Luther was outlawed, thereby losing the protections of citizenship. Even so, Luther could still count on Frederick's protection in Saxony and out into other parts of eastern and northern Germany.

Erasmus played a key part in Luther's protection. In the backroom consultations at Worms, he told Frederick the Wise that Luther's main offense had been against "the bellies of the monks" — a far cry from the complaints of heresy and sedition. Naive and sometimes reckless though he could be politically, Luther was surely aware that Erasmus' 1524 attack not only was a blow to his relations with the humanists but threatened his political protection as well. Opponents of the reform, whether Italian or German, had leaned on Erasmus to write against him for just this reason.

A third source of support in the coalition supporting the Lutheran reform was both more inchoate and volatile politically, but it was just as important. The economy of late-fifteenth-century and early-sixteenth-century Europe was in transition from the feudal system, characteristic of medieval life, to the developing capitalism of the modern period. Mediterranean Europe's famous voyages of discovery around Africa to the Far East and westward to the Americas were a key factor in the change. The voyages themselves required a huge cash outlay. When the spices and precious metals hauled back entered the European marketplace, they broke the barter system that had long characterized rural medieval life, forcing cash exchange. A classic inflationary spiral quickly followed. In order to obtain cash, those who had been lords in the old system attempted to liquefy their assets by forcing the farmers to pay for what they had previously held in common — access to firewood, pasturage, hunting and fishing rights, for example — or gained through the exchange of labor. This resulted in a large migration from the old feudal manors to the developing cities of Germany, some sixty-five of which were designated imperial cities. The dislocation and the economic injustices for those who stayed behind fed a large-scale social unrest that threatened to erupt into conflict. The migrants and the farmers saw Luther's protest as part of their own cause and gave him strong support.

Rural complaints were rising toward a crescendo in the early 1520s, causing considerable fear. With all of the changes underway, early modern Germans considered sedition an ultimate threat. The fear had a basis in fact. Revolt broke into armed conflict in the spring and summer of 1525. With advantages in both armament and leadership, the lords made short work of the farmers — the Peasants' War was quickly over. But the damages, both in loss of life and to property, spilled across Germany.

Luther was caught both ways in the conflict, with loyalties to the nobility who had been his protection and to the farming population that had supported him. Early on, he kept his balance, warning the lords that continued exploitation would have its consequences while admonishing the farmers against turning to force. But when the revolt broke open, Luther turned to the lords to restore order and did so in inflammatory language. *Against the Murdering, Robbing Hoard of Peasants,* his main pronouncement on the matter, could not have been published at a worse time. It hit the streets just when the lords had won the military advantage and appeared to egg them on to further abuse. His later refusal to back down cost him considerably, and has ever since.

8

Luther's statements on the Peasants' War, written while he was considering his reply to Erasmus, indicate the tenor of the times for him. No doubt his share in the fear of sedition characteristic of the times was a factor in his comments. But in fact, the whole situation came replete with apocalyptic overtones. Serving his vocation as a doctor of the church, he had spoken the divine word in the pulpit, at his lecture rostrum, and through the printing press. Widely regarded as a prophet, he had had a prophet's reward. The coalition of humanists, nobility, farmers, and city migrants that had supported him through excommunication and outlawry was breaking down in front of him. The revolt made chaos swirl into the fields and streets in a way that reminded Luther of the book of Genesis's description of the flood, when the bowels of the earth opened. With the eschatological heightening of his reading of Scripture, there was an apocalyptic turn of the times to confirm it for him.

Characteristically, Luther took a couple of steps, one to be anticipated, the other a surprise to everyone else — but in his mind equally logical. As Luther understood it, it was the biblical message of Christ's justifying act — the gospel — that had driven him to this point. So he did what he would do, he went to Scripture to answer Erasmus' arguments. The surprise was that in June of 1525, just when the apocalyptic mess was coming to full boil, Luther got married. Katherine von Bora, most always remembered by her given name and only occasionally as Mrs. Luther, was an escaped nun who had sought Luther's help in contracting a marriage. When two such efforts failed, she suggested offhandedly that he would be an acceptable alternative. To Luther, given the apocalyptic heat, it made eminently good sense at the time to do just that, to take an ordinary responsibility and so to be found in a human position. To Katherine von Bora it made equally good sense for her new husband to reply to Erasmus. She would not have him put down, especially not by the prince of the humanists.

# Competing Theological Frameworks

According to traditional standards, Cajetan was a good Roman Catholic; Erasmus was not. The difference arises out of their relationship to Thomism. Almost two and a half centuries after Thomas' death, Cajetan was still carefully tending the Thomistic categories that the papacy had rendered normative. Erasmus' whole program focused on breaking free of medieval, scholastic speculation to start all over again from ancient wisdom.

For this reason, Erasmus' theological context was not Roman Catholic, as commonly assumed. Traditional Catholics find him as objectionable as Luther, in some ways more so. Rather, his baseline — the grounding metaphors of his theological reflection — were more modern in the historical sense than medieval, more typically Protestant than either Catholic or Lutheran. As a noted Erasmus scholar, John C. Olin, describes him, Erasmus was "a reformer of theology, a reformer of morals, a reformer of the society. The three spheres are intimately connected. The advance of humanist scholarship and the expansion of Christian knowledge are the means whereby the needed reforms will come. . . . Practically the whole corpus of Erasmus' work can be interpreted in this light."[1]

Erasmus reformed theology by clearing away the speculative overgrowth of medieval thought to get down to practical principles; he sought to reform morals by cultivating a simple biblical, personal piety, and he sought the larger reform of society particularly through the reforming movements that sprung up after him in the Upper Rhine valley. His German and Swiss students, such as Ulrich Zwingli in Zurich and John Oecolampadius in Basel, carried forward his program, laying the foundations for modern Protestantism.

An experienced polemicist, Erasmus had an eye for Luther's presuppositions, the basic premises by which an argument stands or falls.

1. *Christian Humanism and the Reformation: Selected Writings of Erasmus with the Life of Erasmus by Beatus Rhenanus,* ed. John C. Olin (New York: Fordham University Press, 1975), p. 11.

So in the *Diatribe,* he went after two issues which he regarded as decisive for Luther. One involved hermeneutics, the assumptions informing the interpretation of Scripture. The other was the relationship between God's sovereignty and human autonomy, the freedom of the will.

Luther had pitched the prior authority of Scripture against the hierarchical ranking of authorities encapsulating all of life. God's Word relativizes every human word, he argued, the gospel literally creating what it requires. Erasmus argued that the Scripture is ambiguous, requiring interpretation. Serving up a variety of troublesome biblical passages to establish this point, Erasmus argued further that given the ambiguity, a variety of interpretations always remains possible. Therefore, he concluded, an authoritative teaching office is necessary to set interpretative limits and determine the essential truths of the faith.

Making this argument, Erasmus brought forward a traditional theory of interpretation dating back to St. Augustine in the early medieval church and before him to Origen, the Alexandrian catechist, who in the third century laid hermeneutical foundations for the church. Invoking Paul's assertion in 1 Corinthians that the "letter kills but the Spirit gives life" — a critically important passage for both Origen and Augustine — this tradition holds that the essential task of the interpreter is to connect the literal meaning of the text with its spiritual import, thereby completing the communication and establishing the biblical truth.

This tradition assumes a concomitant theory of language. Words function by signification, it holds, language calling forth associations that enable the hearer to make the essential connection. When a word and what it signifies are properly aligned, communication occurs. But the alignment can slip, causing ambiguity. The problem may be in the word itself, if it fails to carry its proper significance, or it may be in the hearer, who for one reason or another misses the connection. Either way, the distance between word and meaning remains an essential problem. The interpreter has to overcome the possibilities of ambiguity so that the biblical message, whether doctrinal or moral, can be established.

Power also plays an important part in this way of thinking. The word by itself remains inert, a dead letter that cannot function until its true significance gets unlocked. The disciplines of classical study, including for Erasmus and the humanists in particular in the original languages, release the essential meaning of the text so that it can be applied to the situation at hand. Discovering its meaning, the interpreter gains control of the authority of the text. On the basis of the text, then, the interpreter lays claim to the situation addressed.

Because interpretation involves such power, it must be regulated. Given the inherent problem with ambiguity, not every interpretation is necessarily true or helpful. Thus Erasmus' argument, with the hermeneutical tradition he represents, is closely wedded to the medieval Roman Catholic ecclesiology. As bishop of Rome and so first among equals with all the other bishops, the pope holds the last word in interpretation, using the tradition of the church — the teachings of various church councils, papal declarations, and similar documents — to limit the proper range of interpretation and preserve the truth.

With this, arguing the ambiguity of Scripture against Luther, Erasmus set out the traditional hermeneutic of the church, with its arrangements of power, preserving his place within it. At the same time, he left room for himself and his humanist agenda. Ambiguity is ambiguity, after all — there should always be some room for disagreement.

Erasmus' first main argument is closely correlated with the second, the freedom of the will. If the Scripture is ambiguous, the interpreter must necessarily have within the self the capacity to understand and apply this self to the meaning — either by rejecting or accepting and acting accordingly. Freedom of the will is a defining human characteristic.

Once again, Erasmus stood on the shoulders of ancient Christian tradition, even if he was trying to move it in another direction. Though the language of free will is not biblical — in the absence of direct scriptural reference, it is considered to be implied by a number of texts — the terminology dates back to ancient, Greco-Roman culture. It became a part of the church's vocabulary as the church moved out of its Palestinian origins and established itself in the Mediterranean world.

At one level, freedom of the will has traditionally functioned as a *theologumenon* for the church, that is, as an essential assumption for theological reflection with questionable reference or function beyond thought itself. So in the free will defense, as it is classically called, it is posited that Adam and Eve must have had a free will, the capability, by creation, to accept or reject God's command not to eat of the tree of knowledge in the Garden of Eden. Command by its very nature, as Erasmus argued in bringing this tradition forward against Luther, implies choice. In this way, the assumption of free will serves to explain the presence of sin and its accompanying responsibility.

At this level, where freedom of the will is an essential presupposition in theological logic, virtually the whole medieval tradition was united. In fact, when Luther was excommunicated, his argument in the Heidelberg Disputation that "freedom of the will after the fall, exists in name only" was cited as proof positive of his heresy.

For all of the agreement at this level, however, there was not equal certainty or unanimity about the actual function of the posited free will in relation to God's grace in Christ Jesus, dispensed by the church through the sacraments. On the one side, there were theologians like Pelagius, a contemporary of St. Augustine, and Pelagius' brilliant student, Julian of Eclanum, who argued that reason and willpower are sufficient to moral transformation. Reason understands the requirement of the law, the will applies the self to obedience, and grace provides, at best, some minimal assistance. On the other side were theologians like the older St. Augustine and the later Thomas Aquinas for whom the much greater emphasis on grace proportionately minimized the significance of the will, even if it remained an essential theological assumption. In his last years, for example, Augustine argued that rather than establishing freedom, a sense of choice in the defining relationships of life indicates a disintegration of the will.

Early in the fifth century, with Augustine's lead, the church officially condemned Pelagianism; about a century later, a variant known as Semi-Pelagianism was also anathematized. If free will is an essential assumption of the Catholic tradition, grace is not simply an alternative — both must be given their due. Thomas, who in the course of his studies discovered the condemnation of Semi-Pelagianism, later revised his thinking to set out a synthesis of the will and grace that gave an increasingly strong emphasis to actual grace, grace freely given by God.

While his precise relationship to Pelagianism can be debated, Erasmus' humanism certainly inclined him more to the side of human capability. An ardent student of St. Jerome, another contemporary of Augustine, he knew well the range of opinions in the church's traditions concerning nature and grace. Even with the condemnation of Pelagius, Julian, and the variations in their succession, the free will argument still had an essential place in Catholic faith and there had also been room for those who stressed the power of choice. It was a peripheral question, one in which dogmatists like Cajetan and Luther should move with a little more modesty, acknowledging the open-endedness of language and thought.

So Erasmus deployed a whole series of arguments against Luther on this second point. Some of them were quicker and more passing, such as questions about what the peasants might do if they heard of God's graciousness or an argument that the imperative of God's commands implies indicatively the capacity for choice. Some of them were larger and more involved, such as the nature of God's willing. Quick and facile or more carefully considered, Erasmus' arguments were all set out for the same purpose: to disqualify Luther's one-sided emphasis on God's work and to clear out room for human appropriation and cooperation.

Luther's *Bondage of the Will* has generally been considered difficult reading. Because of Erasmus' superior academic standing, Luther carefully followed late medieval methods of debate, stating Erasmus' argument, examining and refuting it point by point before moving on to his own affirmations. In the parlance of contemporary debate, he went over unto Erasmus' ground, following the course of his opponent's arguments while meticulously examining every point. For this reason, the real force of Luther's argument does not emerge until the last chapter. Close students of the book, including Gerhard Forde, have commonly suggested that it should be read backward, moving from the last chapter through the proceeding, one by one to the first, so that the forest will not get lost in the trees.

As has often been emphasized, Luther was not a Lutheran but a Catholic, through and through. But his way of thinking theologically, his method, was very different. It put him immediately at odds with Erasmus, Cajetan, and Catholic theologians of his own time but also eventually with many of the Lutherans who followed him and with the Protestant tradition that arose out of Erasmus' lineage.

The larger Christian tradition begins theologically with creation and the fall. There are certain inherent human characteristics, present by creation, that distinguish humanity from the other creatures of the earth, such as reason and freedom of the will. These powers function in the context of God's all-embracing law, also inherent to the creation, promoting obedience or turning in the fall toward disobedience. Self-seeking, the force of disobedience, has become the condition of created humanity since the fall, releasing the forces of disorder implicated in the fall. God acted in Christ to restore fallen humanity to its proper obedience so as to save both creature and creation.

Karl Rahner, the greatest Roman Catholic theologian of the twentieth century, recognized a fundamental problem with this way of thinking, a problem that also troubled Luther. Rahner called it "extrinsicism." In the traditional method, the basic powers necessary to rectify the fall are all present prior to the gracious work of Christ Jesus. Reason and will are intrinsic, grace extrinsic, an extra added to fix a system that should have been able to work, conceivably could have worked, without it.

In such a way of thinking, the issue will always be as it was between Pelagius and Augustine (and later became with Erasmus) — How much grace is really needed? Julian of Eclanum was one of the few who identify themselves as Christians who said, "as little as possible." Properly disciplined by the law, willing the good, the believer already has the capacity for moral transformation. Troubled by this, Augustine answered contrariwise, "as much as possible," turning in his *Contra Julianum* to a doctrine of double predestination. Either way, the two are united in their assumptions and share essentially a common method.

Caught in the crucible formed by his own struggles in relation to the biblical word, especially the Psalms and Paul's letters, Luther worked out a different way of thinking theologically. Instead of working ontologically, with assumptions about the creation and inherent characteristics of being, he thought relationally. Thus instead of working from creation and fall to redemption, in effect he works backward from Christ's death and resurrection to what must be assumed, and then forward to what is implied in light of the relationship with creation and creature so established. Rather than proceeding progressively, developmentally, or sequentially, he thought in what has sometimes been called a "circular" manner, such that Christ's justifying is the center or hub and implications necessitated by the triune God's act in Christ radiate from the center like spokes from the hub. In this way, Christ's person and work become the first premise in every theological argument.

Christ Jesus is thus the one true and only intrinsic center, the one "in whom all things hold together," as Paul states, quoting the ancient Christ hymn. All other theological assumptions could be called extrinsic in the sense that they are correlates or consequences required by God's gracious act. At the center of everything is a person, Jesus of Nazareth whom God raised from the dead, not an idea, a system of rules and regulations, or a sequence of causes.

It should be noted that this way of thinking is literally "from faith to faith." Though Luther's arguments concerning the assumptions required or the implications to be drawn are often descriptive or experiential, and tellingly so, they are not detached observation. They view human experience in the light of what Christ has done. He was not advocating a philosophical or theological system in relation to other such systems of thought. He worked at a prior, more fundamental level in which the decisive issue is God's actual dealing *pro me, pro nobis,* for me and for us. It is a "theology of the cross" which exposes every other way of thinking as a theology of glory. A theologian of the cross is driven by God's actual way of relating to us *sub contrario,* under the sign of the opposite in Christ's death and so his resurrection. Glory, on the other hand, attempts to control and domesticate God by fitting him to human assumptions.

So, when Luther took up the hermeneutical argument Erasmus made against him, he did not begin with a theory of language, be it significative or performative. Rather, he began with the assumption common to the church's treatment of Scripture, now radicalized by his own apocalyptic hope: it is God's own Word, God's speech. In the narratives, in the contradictions, in the hiddenness and obscurities that can be seen to mark all of God's dealings with sinful humanity in light of the cross, God in Christ is making himself known as the one at work in every moment.

Thinking this way, Luther acknowledged without hesitation that there are passages in Scripture that are obscure, requiring the services of interpreters. There is a whole realm of biblical language which is, in fact, significative. The law signifies, setting out what God requires in terms of human behavior and attitudes. But the actor in these words is neither the church nor the pious individual seeking to fulfill what the law signifies; the actor, the ultimate speaker, is God, constraining, demanding, confronting, accusing, taking on rebellious creatures seeking above all to be their own gods, especially religiously. Thus where there are obscurities, they are readily clarified by the Scripture itself.

But the clarity of Scripture is not a human project. It is christocentric. "Christ is the Lord of Scripture," Luther writes, then asking, "Take Christ out of Scripture and what do you have left?" To be sure, there are books like Esther, a story of heroism in the face of power, or the letter of James, moral instruction with a passing formulaic reference, in which Christ Jesus is not clearly set forth. But in the light of Christ's death and resurrection, in the light of the overwhelming clarity of the books always given primacy in the church, the whole of the Scripture's message becomes transparently clear. For this reason, it does not require the services of an interpreter but, instead, interprets all attempts at interpretation. The final interpreter, then, is not the scholar, the preacher, or the piety of the pious, but the Spirit of the risen Christ using human words to breathe God's creative power into a broken world.

Luther's argument on the bound will moved in the same fashion. Devastatingly simple, the underlying argument works like this: If Christ's death and resurrection are the sole sufficient cause for justification, there can be no capacity in the human heart or will which could accomplish this. To put it in Jesus' own words, "whoever commits sin is a slave of sin," John 8:34. This first premise and the required conclusion then became the basis for a closely observed description of how appetite functions to bind the desirer to the object of its desires.

With this, Luther made an additional argument more theological in the literal sense of the term. Again, pared down its basics, the argument proceeds simply from the actual event of God's self-giving apprehended in faith. In the preached word and the administered sacrament, God bestows the gifts of the gospel now and for the future. If it is going to deliver on such promises, the certainty of faith itself, then God must be in control of all related events and the unfolding of every moment. That is, if the declaration of the forgiveness of sins actually holds, if in baptism God really does render the last judgment, if in the Lord's Supper Christ Jesus really does bestow his very self, then God must work all in all.

There is room in Luther's argument to speak of relationships in human life where choice does have some power. In "things below us," as he put it, that is, in aspects of life where creatures really do have the control necessary to make legitimate choices, the will functions accordingly — so politics, so personal habits, and the like. But in the definitive relationships of life, such as marriage and the family, choice loses its preeminence to other forces like love and hope that have a power and an integrity of their own. So lovers do not speak of their relationship as a project or an achievement, but describe themselves as having "fallen" in love or been caught up in something greater than themselves. Faith is another matter entirely. In relationship to the God who creates out of nothing, who raised Jesus from the dead, choice is exposed for what it really is, pretense and obstacle. In faith, the triune God is both author and finisher.

Given the nature of the arguments, scholars have been tempted to ascribe the confrontation between Erasmus and Luther to differences of character. Warren Quanbeck, of the Luther Seminary faculty, often commented that Erasmus does theology like a man lying on the brow of a hill, overlooking a warm, sunny valley spreading out below; Luther like a man crawling through that valley in the dark, during a storm. In his biography of Erasmus, Roland Bainton contrasts Erasmus' aloofness and distance with Luther's participation. In earlier years, Forde spoke tellingly of the difference between a playboy and a lover, the playboy seeking the techniques necessary to conquer, the lover lost in the qualities of the beloved. Suggestive and even instructive though they may be, such comparisons reduce to psychology what Luther took as divine necessity. If the God preached in the biblical word acts as declared in actual fact, then situational or characterological differences are, in the end, irrelevant. There is just one thing left: preaching.

Erasmus himself certainly recognized the stakes in his exchange with Luther. The *Bondage of the Will* struck him with unanticipated force. What he had offered as a marginal correction came back against him in a full-scale assault that left him publicly exposed and grasping. He spent the next several years working on a reply that, when published, came to something over eight hundred pages. For all of his effort, he was not able to dislodge Luther's case against him. The *Diatribe* and the *Bondage of the Will* have been locked together ever since as formative statements of the Reformation.

## The State of the Question

One of the most important historical examinations of the Erasmus-Luther debate was published in 1969 by Harry J. McSorley under a not-so-helpful title provided by the American publishers, *Luther Right or Wrong?* A demitted Paulist priest and a devout Thomist, McSorely was one of the leading participants in a Roman Catholic reappraisal of Luther seeking footings for ecumenical reconciliation among the churches.

Surveying the history of the argument with meticulous and extended precision, McSorley wrote the traditional Roman Catholic reply to Luther that Cajetan might have offered if he, rather than Erasmus, had had the opportunity to challenge Luther publicly. He argued for a convergence between Thomas and Luther on the first of the arguments for the bound will as the slavery of sin. But McSorley also held that Luther's argument concerning divine necessity places him outside the Roman Catholic tradition.

Along the way, treating the ecumenical prospects for Lutheran–Roman Catholic bilateral conversations then promisingly underway, McSorley provided extensive evidence to show the subsequent Lutheran abandonment of Luther's position. His assessment was accurate at the time and has remained so. Lutheran theologians, including many leading Luther scholars, have backed away. And what is true in the scholarly community is even more so popularly. In the corrosive reduction worked by the American melting pot, with few exceptions, Lutherans have become indistinguishable from their generic Protestant counterparts for whom free choice, the decision of the will, is the hallmark of true faith.

McSorely mentions a German scholarly exception, a theologian little known in the United States and Canada, even in scholarship, but who has nevertheless had a profound influence on a few: Hans Joachim Iwand. Gustaf Wingren, himself a great Swedish Luther scholar and theologian, once described Iwand as the best Lutheran theologian of the twentieth century. In Wingren's estimation, Iwand, who was a close friend and associate of Karl Barth, tempered his Lutheranism through Barth's critique without losing his confessional integrity. Iwand spent much of the Second World War in prison for his opposition to Hitler, and since the war has unfortunately remained obscure to most students of theology in America, including Lutherans.

Early on in Forde's work, he was gripped by two principle sources: Barth's *Romans Commentary,* one of Barth's most important early theological works, and Luther's *Bondage of the Will.* His copies of the two volumes, the Oxford University Press translation of the *Romans* and Packer's and Johnston's translation of Luther, are dog-eared and battered with constant use. Forde's primary intellectual companion in this tension between Luther and Barth was Iwand. At the turning point of the argument in Forde's major publications, Iwand invariably provides the warrant. Lauri Haikola, a great Finnish Luther scholar, holds the same position in Forde's thinking for his historical work.

Like McSorely, Forde also played a part in Lutheran–Roman Catholic dialogues in America. For over twenty-five years, he participated in the conversations, finding his closest companionship with some of the most conservative Catholics. In the end, what Steven Ozment of Yale University once called "the Romantic school" — an ecumenism seeking a vision of convergence by obscuring long-standing historical differences — took over the conversations. Represented among Lutherans by people like George Lindbeck and more vociferously but without formal standing by Robert W. Jenson and Carl Braaten, this school took over the ecumenical offices of the Evangelical Lutheran Church in America.

Romantic movements always create philistines, whether their leaders are qualified for the positions or not. Forde was dismissed from the conversations for not sharing "the vision."

Douglas John Hall of McGill University in Montreal, who has also had a long-term interest in Iwand, has described the theology of the cross as a thin tradition, generally found at the margins. That is where Forde has worked, both in his church and Luther Seminary, St. Paul, and now in his retirement. But from this position, he, like Iwand, has maintained an extensive influence. Among scholars, Donald H. Juel, late of Princeton Theological Seminary, was an outstanding example. A younger generation, including Steven Paulson of Luther Seminary and Mark Mattes of Grandview College, Des Moines, is now taking over his work including collections of Forde's essays and lectures. But Forde's real legacy has been with preachers caught in the predicaments of parish ministry and seeking above all, faithful proclamation.

This book is in some ways a set of meditations. Though the work is closely informed historically, Forde has for the most part dropped the normal apparatus of academic theology — the footnotes and the like — to concentrate on particular passages in the *Bondage of the Will* which open up the whole argument. Standing on Luther's shoulders, he is bringing forward the arguments that register their theological impact in proclamation and witness.

When Barth was working up his *Church Dogmatics* during summers in the Swiss Alps, he wrote to a friend that he had to guard himself every moment from slipping back into the old way of making the self both center and standard. The gospel is antithetical to the whole human enterprise, the attempt to become self-creating. As is to be expected, Forde has continued the same struggle in the writing of this volume. The gospel's character and Luther's circular way of thinking can be baffling, even to someone who has spent a lifetime immersed in the sources, but Forde has always managed in his writing and preaching to fight from the rough edges to gain clarity by confessing, "If you begin with the assumption of freedom, the preoccupation is always how to keep freedom in check, how to bind; But if you begin with the assumption of bondage, the preoccupation is always how to set out the word that frees."

*Chapter One*

---

# The Argument about Scripture

*If any one text defeats free choice, its numberless forces will profit it nothing.*

LW 33:161

Fundamental to the argument over free choice is the question of the interpretation and authority of Scripture. Both Luther and Erasmus agreed that Scripture should be the arbiter in the dispute. Nevertheless, Luther complained that Erasmus did not stick strictly to the agreement because he insisted on calling the fathers, martyrs, holy men and women, and so on, to bear witness to the truth of his argument. Luther suspected Erasmus of expanding his argument beyond Scripture in this way in order to belittle Luther's argument by comparison. What could a little-known professor from a third-rate university out in the backwaters of the empire count against the great tradition and the mighty Erasmus? (Packer, 62).

But the real problem came immediately to the fore in the fact that Luther understood the argument from Scripture in a manner radically different from that of Erasmus, and, we shall have to say, different from most modern exegetes ever since. Erasmus seems to have thought scriptural argument was a matter of collecting passages and authorities for and against the issue at hand and then weighing them and totaling up the

23

"box score." It was a kind of "word study" method. The number of times a word occurs in a treatise is supposed to be of decisive import for its interpretation. Luther, however, was not at all persuaded or moved by such methods. The epigraph over this chapter leaves little doubt. Numbers do not and cannot settle the matter of powers of the will. If there were only one passage, one text against free choice, that single occurrence would be decisive. Characterizing Erasmus' method, Luther says:

> [A]fter having marshaled innumerable passages of Scripture like a very formidable army in support of free choice (in order to inspire courage in the confessors and martyrs and all the saints of both sexes on the side of free choice, and fear and trembling in all those who deny and sin against free choice), she [that is, the *Diatribe*] pretends there is only a contemptible little rabble against free choice, and actually allows only two passages [the hardening of Pharaoh's heart and the choice of Jacob over Esau]. (LW 33:161)

Note carefully the language. Luther sees the controversy not as polite academic discourse but rather as a desperate battle. He suspects that the forces marshaled by Erasmus are intended not merely to inform but eventually to provoke fear and trembling in the "contemptible little rabble" foolish enough to attack free choice.

Thus the nature of Luther's argument about Scripture and its authority begins to emerge. He is not interested merely in what Scripture says but in what it does, how it functions in the argument over free choice. We are dealing in these matters with "fear and trembling," with matters concerning what Luther called "the conscience." In such matters one passage is enough to shatter confidence and send one on the road to despair, one's hopes scattered to the winds. A simple question is all it takes: "Are you one of the elect? Do you *really, sincerely* believe?" Have you actually "done what is in you," as the Nominalists would say? And so on without end. A confident answer is not readily forthcoming. It can never be easily taken for granted. That is why just one passage can destroy confidence resting on innumerable passages asserting free choice.

## The Argument about Scripture

It is obvious from this opening discussion that the argument about Scripture leads to deeper dimensions of the faith. The claim that one passage is enough to "shake the foundations" of a faith built on free choice is likely only where reverence toward Scripture as Word of God is already present, at least in some form. Only on such a basis could Luther and Erasmus argue on common ground. But that is just the problem. Erasmus set out to win a debate. Luther sought to comfort and rescue the lost.

Do they, in fact, argue on common ground? The debate sparked by Erasmus' ensuing argument about assertions in theology and the clarity of Scripture cracks the debate open. A few sentences by way of historical background will help to make this clear.

The argument about assertions had been heating up in the disputes of 1515 and subsequent years. It was fanned into flame by the notorious Bull of Leo X (*Exsurge Domine,* June 1520) threatening Luther with excommunication. In the Bull, Leo had attacked Luther's "assertions." Prominent among these were "assertions" having to do with free choice and "doing what was in one." Luther had "asserted" that since the fall free choice has been a "mere title" that does not exist in reality, that anyone who seeks to "do what is in him" commits mortal sin, and that all things happen by divine necessity. There was no set of assertions, of course, so much designed to upset and enrage the "theologians" as these — be they scholastic or humanist. They struck at the heart of the Roman theological system. But Luther held his ground and responded to Pope Leo with further "assertions" in a treatise entitled *Assertion on all the Articles of Martin Luther Recently Condemned by the Bull of Leo X.*

At this point Erasmus was finally persuaded to enter the lists. So the battle began in earnest. First we look briefly at the Erasmian position. It is, for the most part, an attempt to establish a viable scriptural position on the matter before the house. But Erasmus finds, like his followers today, that Scripture is not really up to the task. For an Erasmian, Scripture appears to confuse matters more than to solve them. Showing his humanist reserve, Erasmus declared himself to be uneasy with "assertions" and sought rather the coolness of abstractions and the academic discussion. He did not realize, apparently, that the assertions were *confessions*

25

for Luther — matters of faith and conscience — about which there could be, in the end, no doubt. Doubt about these innermost matters exposed one to the assaults and terrors of the adversary. Doubt in these matters meant, for Luther, *eo ipso* the absence of salvation. If there was doubt about these innermost matters there could be no salvation.

Luther was perfectly aware that there are many things about which one might be skeptical. There are unprofitable doctrines, useless opinions, and minor issues about which one is at liberty to doubt. But it is quite another matter if one is dealing with essential truths, with confessions upon which faith itself rests. Thus Luther can say that to take no pleasure in assertions and not to delight in them cannot possibly be a Christian position. "Take away assertions and you take away Christianity. Why, the Holy Spirit is given to the Christian from heaven in order that he may glorify Christ and confess Him even unto death" (LW 33:21). Indeed, the Spirit asserts to such purpose that he breaks in upon the whole world and convinces it of sin as if challenging it to battle. Erasmus' skeptical reserve simply will not do in matters of conviction and conscience. So Luther concluded his opening section with the famous words, "The Holy Spirit is no skeptic, and the things He has written in our hearts are not doubts or opinions, but assertions — surer and more certain than sense and life itself" (LW 33:24).

Here we have the first indication of a major divide. For Luther God the Spirit is the active "player" in this drama. God acts through the Scriptures. The Scriptures are the Word of God, that is, they are not, as for Erasmus, mere words about God, but the Word from God. Mere words about God will be of a quite different sort and function than words from God. It is the burden of the argument in the *Bondage of the Will* that words about bondage intend to dominate and take control of the relationship. They inevitably take the shape of a defense mechanism against God. Scripture is treated as though it were material suitable for making a theory about the proper relationship between God and humans. This theory is then thought to be put into practice when human beings accept it and try to live according to it. But this is false theology in Luther's view, a theology of glory. Humans remain in control according to such a theory. Scripture becomes our tool by which we bring God

26

to heel. The theory is used to make God our debtor. But then we are caught in the trap of our own making. It is as Isaac Singer was once heard to say, "We must believe in free will, we have no choice!" The drive toward freedom of choice ends in bondage. It is not the task of theology to construct a theory of God that is supposed to win us over by attractiveness. It is the business of theology to foster the preaching of the Word of God.

We can therefore see that a major parting of the ways begins to announce itself already in the interpretation of Scripture and in the argument about assertions. It is hardly surprising to find that the opponents disagree on Scripture itself. Erasmus wants to use Scripture to build his theory. Since this theory is rooted in claims of free choice Erasmus cannot but find Scripture ambiguous and contradictory. Some passages in it appear to be for free choice and some appear to be against it. What is to be done? The interpreter must come to the rescue. The interpreter must go to work on the text to resolve the alleged contradictions. For Luther, as we shall see, it is just the opposite. The text goes to work on the interpreter to do what it talks about.

It is consequent, therefore, that the argument about Scripture should take the form of a battle over the *claritas,* the clarity, of Scripture. This means, of course, that the fault is attributed to Scripture, not to the interpreter. The question, putatively, is whether Scripture is unclear, not whether the interpreter is unclear! The difficulty in the whole procedure lies in the fact that Scripture does not deliver "the goods" sufficient to turn the free choice theory into reality. The "scheme" drives only to a collision. To save the theory one must claim that the ambiguity is the fault of Scripture, not the fault of the interpreter. Interpreters of an Erasmian type are driven to take refuge in the Scriptures' supposed lack of clarity. Where one encounters passages casting doubt on free choice or rejecting it altogether one must take refuge in tropes, figures of speech that end up explaining those passages away. What Luther was doing with Scripture is a symbolic interpretation, not allegorical. The allegorical is an exegetical trick used when one already knows what the text means, but uses a trope to escape the text and preserve the initial theory in the face of clear words to the contrary.

27

The general theory touted by Erasmus is the familiar moralistic one: If the will operates by necessity then everything is threatened by determinism. In that case, guilt cannot be assigned and striving for good cannot be rewarded. All passages in Scripture demanding choice or response are pointless and ridiculous if there is not some degree of freedom. The very fact that God has given us laws presupposes some power to respond to their demands, or else it is a mockery and nonsense. Furthermore, God is in the highest measure unjust if he imposes necessity on us and subsequently punishes us for deeds we could not avoid. Scripture simply will not support such a "theory," and so on and so on.

But where God is the actor Scripture cannot be used in Erasmian fashion. The interpreter, Luther insists, is not given license to construct self-satisfying and pleasing theories about our relation to God by ironing out the supposedly unclear wrinkles in the text. The reason for such procedure is simply to make room for the freedom of the will. I take it that is why Luther speaks of a twofold lack of clarity and a double lack of light. Clarity becomes an issue, Luther maintains, because it is the interpreter who is unclear — not the Scripture. The interpreter, therefore, must be called to account before the Scripture. The reason for the twofold unclarity is that when the would-be interpreter sets out to find room for the freedom of choice he misreads both himself and the scriptural Word. The interpreter attempts to overpower Scripture and so stifles its message. Luther uses the idea of a twofold clarity (and the lack of it) in analyzing the problem.

The first sort of clarity Luther called the "external" clarity of Scripture. External clarity has to do with Luther's insistence that Scripture is crystal clear over against the Erasmian claim of ambiguity. When Luther speaks of external clarity he generally refers to the ministry of the Word and the basic doctrine and narrative of the church — the Scriptures, creeds, sacred history, and so forth. He refers to this as "the subject matter" of the church's witness. He means the "what" of the message, and insists that it is in itself perfectly clear. This means that "the profoundest mysteries of the supreme Majesty are no more hidden away. . . . 'The veil remains on their heart,'" 2 Corinthians 3:15 (Packer, 72).

The fact that obscurity still "veils" the meaning of some texts is due not to lack of clarity in the texts but rather to our "ignorance of their terms" or "ignorance of their vocabulary or grammar." Once again we see that even on the level of the "external" clarity Luther refuses to lay the blame for whatever lack of clarity may emerge on Scripture. It is due rather to ignorance of grammar and/or laziness in exegetical effort.

But the second dimension of the clarity problem is the source of even more trouble. This Luther refers to as the "internal clarity" of Scripture and has to do with the understanding of the heart. Here we return to what was only hinted at earlier: that we need the Holy Spirit not because the Scriptures are so unclear but rather because they are so clear! Thus Luther could say,

> If you speak of the internal clarity, no man perceives one iota of what is in the Scriptures unless he has the Spirit of God. All men have a darkened heart, so that even if they can recite everything in Scripture and know how to quote it, yet they apprehend nothing of it. They neither believe in God, nor that they themselves are creatures of God, nor anything else, as Psalm 13 [14:1] says: "The fool has said in his heart, 'There is no God.'" For the Spirit is required for the understanding of Scripture, both as a whole and in any part of it. If on the other hand, you speak of the external clarity, nothing at all is left obscure or ambiguous, but everything there is in the Scriptures has been brought out by the Word into the most definite light, and published to all the world. (LW 33:28)

It goes without saying that such words are offensive to most modern exegetes and interpreters. Everyone knows that Scripture is full of ambiguity and contradiction — ostensibly . . . ! Perhaps if we try an example we can divine Luther's meaning. Take the infamous words about which there is much argument with Erasmus later. God says, "I will harden the heart of Pharaoh." Luther's point seems to be that taken at face value the words are perfectly clear and simple. They manifest an "external clarity." There is nothing grammatically or linguistically difficult about them. Aside from the name Pharaoh there is only one word of

*[margin handwritten note: Scripture is clear — but we try to impose "free will" on to it]*

29

more than a syllable. The fact is, however, that we have much difficulty with such passages. Why? Because we do not like what they say! We are, so to speak, internally torn apart by the words. And so we twist and turn in attempts to make them say something other than they quite clearly do say. Usually that turns out to be some variation of "free will" theology in which the subject and object are switched around and everything turned upside down. Pharaoh does the choosing and God has to wait upon him. Ultimately Pharaoh is in charge of the Exodus. But even more seriously, Luther points out, God is dethroned and the creature denies his or her creatureliness.

So Luther could say that unless one has the Spirit of God one does not perceive one iota of what is in the Scriptures. One may have a grasp of the external clarity and be able to quote profusely and learnedly, and yet because there is no sense for the internal clarity, one does not understand what Scripture is about at all. Such a person "sees" in the flight from Pharaoh perhaps a political struggle, or an economic one (with perhaps a suggestion of racial overtones), but not what the Spirit of God teaches.

Here we catch a glimpse of what Luther meant in the *Heidelberg Disputation* in saying that a theologian of glory calls the bad good and the good bad, while a theologian of the cross says what a thing is. Luther is concerned with what the Word of God as "Living Word" actually does when it invades our lives, our experience, our space.

# Chapter Two

# The Argument about God

*This gouty foot laughs at your doctoring.*

LW 33:53

*The Bondage of the Will* arouses much incredulity, dismay, anxiety, and outright anger when we hear what Luther has to say about God. God rules all things by immutable necessity. So says Luther. To be sure, Luther did not like the philosophical and scholastic terminology in which the argument was couched, particularly words like "necessity," "immutability," "fate," "force," "foreknowledge," and so forth. In ordinary parlance such words imply that we are like puppets being jerked around against our wills by a malevolent master puppeteer. Nevertheless, Luther sails steadfastly into the maelstrom brought on by the actual words and the doctrine of God the argument engenders. We shall look at Luther's argument a bit later. First we need to look briefly at the Erasmian position regarding God.

Erasmus' position reflects at bottom the same dreary moralism touted by everyone from the lowliest neophyte to the most learned professor. People worry endlessly, in countless subtle ways and often with touching piety, that grace is going to upset the moral applecart, or perhaps that they will lose control over their destiny. The differences among them are merely matters of degree. In other words, Erasmus' view on free choice is the common stock of virtually everyone who thinks on the matter, from believer to unbeliever, saint to sinner, theologian to philosopher. Indeed, Luther even tried to excuse himself for not replying to Erasmus right away by claiming that Erasmus had said nothing new! If God rules all things by immutable necessity, so the argument goes, both morality and theodicy are undercut. Who would lead a moral life? Who would reform his life? How could our works be meritorious? Who could love such a God with all her heart, a God who condones and apparently wills the suffering of the innocent?

Furthermore, and perhaps of most gravity for Erasmus' method, he held that there were some things that were better reserved for the learned and dispassionate discussion of the schools and universities. They ought not be published where they would vex and trouble the "common herd" (Erasmus' own words in LW 33:45). Thus, for Erasmus, even if it were true that God rules all things by immutable necessity, it would be better not to let the "common herd" in on such lofty and dangerous academic secrets. It would only cause violence, upheaval, war, and bloodshed. Some diseases, Erasmus opined, are better borne than their cure. A wise physician will know how best to moderate the proper cure.

Luther was infuriated by such exegetical imperialism that allowed Erasmus to persist in his opinion that the doctrine of the bondage of the will was among those doctrines that ought not be put on public display before the unlearned. Erasmus persisted in his opinion that the doctrine of the bondage of the will was among those doctrines that ought not be put on public display before the unlearned. For Luther, Erasmus once again plays the role of the zealous and pious preacher who holds back on grace to make sure that morality will be served! This was of fundamental importance for Luther. In fact, he called the proper knowledge of what God does in relation to human free will a good one-half of the Christian "summa" (system of Christian dogma).

Some of the argumentation is worth repeating to get a feeling for the flavor and urgency of the debate. When Erasmus holds that it is unnecessary, irreverent, inquisitive, and superfluous for the "average" person to be bothered about the bondage of the will, Luther is enraged. The

Erasmian position simply persists in its view that the first concern is morality rather than larger issues of faith, reverence before God, and the deeper dimensions of the Christian life under the cross. The laity can concern themselves with moral reform while the professors debate abstract theological issues! — a familiar procedure in the life of the church, alas, even down to the present day. Luther's fury was heightened by Erasmus' statement on the "sum" of the Christian life:

> So in my opinion, as far as free choice is concerned, what we have learnt from Holy Writ is this: if we are in the way of true religion we should eagerly press on to better things, forgetting the things that are behind; if we are entangled in sins, we should strive with all our might, have recourse to the remedy of penitence and entreat by all means the mercy of the Lord, without which no human will or endeavor is effective; and whatever is evil in us, let us impute to ourselves, whatever is good let us ascribe wholly to the divine benevolence, to which we owe our very being; then for the rest, let us believe that whatever befalls us in this life, whether joyful or sad, it has been sent by God for our salvation, and that no wrong can be done to anyone by him, who by nature is just, even if some things happen that we feel we have not deserved, nor should anyone despair of forgiveness from a God who is by nature most merciful. (LW 33, note 27)

These are, of course, very pious, high-sounding, and appealing words. But Luther found them shockingly vacuous as a description of Christian faith. Why? Because there is nothing particularly Christian about them! There is no mention of Christ's distinctive work, nor is there mention of the Spirit. It is a draft of the Christian faith, Luther says, "which any Jew or Gentile totally ignorant of Christ could certainly draw up with ease" (LW 33:29). Hence, they are for Luther, Christless, Spiritless words, chillier than ice (Packer, 75). Erasmus replied that he was giving only what should be enough for "ordinary people" in contrast to the highly debatable and almost inexplicable problems that beset the subject of free choice (Packer, 76). Erasmus doesn't seem to realize that that is precisely the problem! Theologians don't "fix" the God problem by a remodeling job or by whisking him away behind the walls of academia. The attempt to do so only makes matters worse. If Jesus and the Spirit are taken out of the picture the only possible means of divine approach is undercut. A gospel preacher has no common ground with such a procedure.

So we begin to see the point of Luther's pithy saying, "this gouty foot laughs at your doctoring" (LW 33:53). Gout was an excruciatingly painful, and in those days virtually incurable, affliction. It was a disease that just would not yield to the doctors' manipulations. The more the doctors attempted to do something about it, the worse it got.

And so it was for Luther with Erasmus' proposed "treatment" of the problem of free choice versus immutable necessity. Erasmus counsels avoiding the matter. He claimed it to be too difficult and upsetting — indeed irreverent, useless, inquisitive, and superfluous — for the "common herd." He finally concluded, "What is above us does not concern us." In Luther's view, that was Erasmus' solace for the sufferers. We shall see later that Luther too could use the adage but in a radically different sense. Erasmus used it as a defense of free will and the claims of the moral life. One could safely ignore that which is above to concentrate on moral perfection and more "practical" matters. Luther used the adage as a consequence of the God revealed in the preaching of the gospel. Protecting the place of the moral life does not help the stricken conscience. The gouty foot mocks such advice. The desperate pain of guilt, failure, and emptiness remains unhealed.

In effect, Luther's reply to Erasmus' stratagem (which remains basically the same today: ignore the problem!) is to point out that the "common herd" knows all about it already. In the vernacular, Luther's reply to Erasmus was, "Who are you kidding, Erasmus? Everybody knows already, or at least fears or even resents the God who rules all things by necessity and foreknows nothing contingently! The pain of God cannot be removed by theological doctoring. The problem is to get this God off our backs!" The question is, how this is to be done? How is the gouty foot to be healed? One thing is for certain. It is not done by redoing God's "job description." That only makes matters worse.

Before turning to the basic argument in the God-question, Luther

34

asks some subsidiary questions. Why is it, he wants to know, that Christians have so much trouble with the doctrine of God when pagan poets, philosophers, and even common folk have no problems? From this we can see, Luther maintains,

> that the knowledge of God's predestination and foreknowledge remained with the common people no less than the awareness of his existence itself. But those who wished to appear wise went so far astray in their reasonings that their hearts were darkened and they became fools (Rom. 1[:21-22]), and denied or explained away the things that the poets and common people, and even their own conscience, regarded as entirely familiar, certain and true. (LW 33:41)

Luther was adamant about the importance of knowing what power free choice has over against the immutability and foreknowledge of God. This, he could say, was "the cardinal issue." For if God is God it follows that all we do must be subordinate to his will and happen by his necessity. This, for Luther, is the thunderbolt that knocks free will flat and utterly shatters it (LW 33:263). At this point the argument for Luther is a matter of straightforward and hard-nosed logic. If God is asserted to be just and kind must he not be immutably so? All scholastic attempts to make distinctions to ameliorate the crisis of the encounter with almighty God are cast aside.

For instance, consider the distinction between the immutability of God's will over against his foreknowledge. Erasmus apparently wanted to insist on the idea that God's will is immutable but not his foreknowledge. This might give Erasmus room to say that though God's will is immutable, a changeable foreknowledge affords room for change with regard to the future. Luther will have none of it. "God's . . . will is eternal and changeless, because His nature is so." Then Luther simply follows out the logic:

> From which it follows, by resistless logic, that all we do, however it may appear to us to be done mutably and contingently, is in reality done necessarily and immutably in respect of God's will. For the will

35

of God is effective and cannot be impeded, since power belongs to God's nature; and His wisdom is such that He cannot be deceived. (Packer, 80)

Thus Luther moves to plug every loophole that would give free choice a place to assert itself, and answers Erasmus' charge that openly teaching the bondage of the will would yield terrible chaos and devastating warfare:

Let me tell you, therefore — and I beg you to let this sink deep into your mind — I hold that a solemn and vital truth, of eternal consequence, is at stake in this discussion; one so crucial and fundamental that it ought to be maintained and defended even at the cost of life, though as a result the whole world should be, not just thrown into turmoil and uproar, but shattered in chaos and reduced to nothingness. (Packer, 90)

The best known and heftiest battle was (and still is?) around the problem of necessity. Scholastic theologians tried to work with the distinction between the "necessity of consequence" and "the necessity of the thing consequent." If God wills something to come to pass, the necessary consequence is that it come to pass. There is a kind of necessity involved. But it is not a necessity of the thing consequent; that is, God is under no necessity to bring it to pass. Were there such necessity, it would be a necessity of the thing consequent. If God, that is, wills to create a world, then it necessarily comes to be. But God is under no absolute necessity to create that world. That would be determinism. But the distinction intends to allow for a kind of necessity at the same time as it makes room for a little bit of free choice. Luther dismisses the distinction as being patently ridiculous. All it establishes is that the thing consequent is not god! And that we knew already. The gouty foot is not healed by scholastic distinctions.

To be sure, Luther does have some reservations about the use of the word "necessity" in the discussion of free choice. He wishes there were a better word. Necessity carries with it too much the notion of compulsion and is inappropriate to describe willing, either in God or humans.

"For neither the divine nor the human will does what it does, whether good or evil, under any compulsion but from sheer pleasure or desire, as with true freedom; and yet the will of God is immutable and infallible and it governs our mutable will . . ." (LW 33:39). An exceedingly important text! We shall have to return to it later. For now it is enough to note that it shows clearly that the bondage of the will in question is not, for Luther, a matter of force or determinism. No one is forced. It is something more like an addiction. We all do what we want to do! That is precisely our bondage. We are not jerked around by a transcendent puppeteer. Luther appeals to the reader's intelligence to supply what the word "necessity" ought to convey:

> The reader's intelligence must therefore supply what the word "necessity" does not express, by understanding it to mean what you might call the immutability of the will of God and the impotence of our evil will, or what some have called the necessity of immutability, though this is not very good either grammatically or theologically. (LW 33:39)

Having dispensed with some typical attempts to find loopholes in divine necessity we turn to Luther's main argument. Why, we might well ask, does Luther insist so adamantly on the immutability of God when it seems to undermine both faith and morals? As Erasmus asked, "Who will be good? Who will change his life?" and so forth. Reflected in the Erasmian position is evidence of more concern for the morals of the "common herd" than anything else. Luther was of a completely different mind:

> Who will take pains to correct his life? I answer: No man will and no man can, for God cares nothing for your correctors without the Spirit, since they are hypocrites. But the elect and the godly will be corrected by the Holy Spirit, while the rest perish uncorrected. Augustine does not say that no man's or all men's good works are crowned, but that some men's are. So there will be some who correct their life.

37

Who will believe, you say, that he is loved by God? I answer: No man will or can believe this; but the elect will believe while the rest perish in unbelief, indignant, and blaspheming as you are here. So some will believe.

As to your saying that a window is opened for impiety by these dogmas, let it be so; such people belong to the above-mentioned leprosy of evil that must be endured. Nevertheless, by these same dogmas there is opened at the same time a door to righteousness, an entrance to heaven and a way to God for the godly and the elect. (LW 33:60-61)

What can Luther mean by these strange and offensive words? Careful attention must be paid because they indicate once again that Luther thinks about these matters in quite a different fashion from that of Erasmus and the vast majority of interpreters down to the present day. For Erasmus the fact that God "runs the show" according to his immutable foreknowledge is destructive of faith and morals. God becomes a frightening ogre who must be brought to heel, made "nice" by the interpreter. As Luther put it to Erasmus,

> To talk as you do, one must imagine the Living God to be nothing but a kind of shallow and rather ignorant ranter declaiming from some platform, whose words you can if you wish interpret in any direction you like, and accept or reject them accordingly as ungodly men are seen to be moved or affected by them. And: it was here you should have put your finger to your lips in reverence for what lay hidden, and adoring the secret counsels of the majesty you should have cried with Paul: "O man, who art thou that contendest with God?" (LW 33:60)

For one who thinks as Erasmus does, the immutability of God which seems to cancel out "free choice" is detrimental to faith and morals. Indeed, it makes them impossible. For Luther the matter is just the opposite. The divine immutability is what makes faith possible. How, after all, can we be certain of salvation? If God does not rule by his immutable necessity, who, Luther asks, will believe his promises? Luther, that is, goes directly to the divine immutability as the basis for faith's certainty. How do we know? Faith is grasped, captivated by the revealed God. In baptism, for instance, God has promised! It has happened! It is revealed! And God does not lie. His promises are immutable. Faith is created and sustained by the promises of God, not by the efforts of free choice. This is a matter of highest importance for faith. As Luther put it:

> I go farther and say, not only how true these things are . . . but also how religious, devout and necessary a thing it is to know them. For if these things are not known there can be neither faith nor any worship of God. For that would indeed be ignorance of God, and where there is such ignorance there cannot be salvation, as we know. For if you doubt or disdain to know that God foreknows all things, not contingently, but necessarily and immutably, how can you believe his promises and place a sure trust and reliance on them? For when he promises anything, you ought to be certain that he knows and is able and willing to perform what he promises; otherwise you will regard him as neither truthful nor faithful, and that is impiety and a denial of the Most High God. But how will you be certain and sure unless you know that he knows and wills and will do what he promises, certainly, infallibly, immutably, and necessarily? And we ought not only to be certain that God wills and will act necessarily and immutably, but also to glory in the fact, as Paul says in Romans 3[:4]: "Let God be true though every man be false." (LW 33:42)

Luther's claim is that if the divine action in, say, baptism is not a carrying out in history of the immutable will of God, it loses its object and thus its certainty. It could be just an "accident" or a matter of social custom, or perhaps just the wish of Grandma! All such contingencies will no doubt be at work but God does all things by immutable necessity, in spite of all the contingencies that appear to be at work. Luther insists that the act, the promise, is the deed of the immutable God. For that is precisely the Christian faith: to believe and trust in the promises of the immutable God, no matter what that may entail, no matter how many contingencies and difficulties may afflict. The immutability of God is the guarantee, the "backup" for the preaching of the gospel. If it happens, it is the will of God! That is the only cure for the gouty foot! If one attempts to effect a "cure" by redoing God, erasing the divine immutability, one simply tears God out of the picture and leaves the believer helpless and hopeless. As Luther put it,

> . . Christian Faith is entirely extinguished, the promises of God and the whole gospel are completely destroyed, if we teach and believe that it is not for us to know the necessary foreknowledge of God and the necessity of the things that are to come to pass. For this is the one supreme consolation of Christians in all adversities, to know that God does not lie, but does all things immutably, and that his will can neither be resisted nor changed nor hindered. (LW 33:43)

We are approaching here Luther's doctrine of the hidden God. We shall have to deal with this more fully later. For the present it is enough to note that Luther sees trust in the revealed God as inherent to faith itself and the only "solution" to the "problem of God." The revealed God is the God of the immutable promise. Thus it bids us stop before the supreme majesty of the hidden God. There seems to be a conundrum when we come to this point. On the one hand Luther insists on the givenness of the hidden God and that it is entirely necessary for faith to grapple with that God. As it is often put, we must know the "what" of the hidden God. But at the same time we cannot know the "why." We must know that God is the immutable one who elects and rejects. We are not running the show. But we cannot know why one and not the other is among the elect. If we knew that we would turn it into a legal system and it would destroy us! Faith in the word of proclamation is the only way. What the revelation tells us is that we cannot know the hidden God. We cannot even know that God is hidden. Hiddenness is, paradoxically, a revealed truth! This should be apparent to us in the cross.

There is considerable confusion about this among theologians of Erasmus' stripe. Erasmus thought the hiddenness involved was mere secrecy, something that could easily be brought into the light of day — like the mysterious Corycian cavern of fame in Greek myth and religion.

From the vantage point of that understanding of hiddenness, Luther is often criticized for knowing too much about the hidden God. The talk of immutability and necessity, for instance, is often taken in this light. The reason for such criticism, however, is patent. The critic seeks holes in the hiddenness so as to insert ideas of human sovereignty and "works righteousness." If the criticism can unseat divine immutability, it can force room for the self to become the subject of all sentences granting salvation. The "I" becomes the lead (and ultimately the only) actor in the story of salvation. One need only listen to today's sermons to see the result of that!

So the picture begins to emerge. Jesus comes into this world only to evoke and reveal hiddenness. No one knows who he is. In Mark's Gospel only the demons recognize him. So he is crucified for his claims. So why this torturous "road to salvation when," as Luther is well aware, "so many evils appear to proceed from them?" Luther begins in his usual fashion by simply asserting that God has willed it and that that ought to be good enough reason for those who fear God. Nevertheless Luther does not stop there but goes on to mention two considerations which demand that such things (and now note carefully!) should be preached. The preaching holds the key, not dogmatic arguments attempting to break through to the hidden majesty and remove what appear to be scandalous offenses. The first consideration is "the humbling of our pride and knowledge of the grace of God, and the second is the nature of Christian faith itself" (LW 33:61).

The humbling of our pride! Luther lays great stress on this throughout *The Bondage of the Will* as well as throughout the rest of his theology. It is our pride over against God that makes us think we can "re-do" God and break in upon him in his hidden majesty to discover why he acts as he does and criticize his actions. "Why," Luther asks Erasmus, "do you not restrain yourself and deter others from prying into things that God has willed to be hidden from us, and has not set forth in the Scriptures?" Humility guards the door to the knowledge of God. With the Augustinian tradition anchored in 1 Peter 5:5 Luther holds that God has "assuredly promised his grace to the humble, those who lament and despair of themselves" (LW 33:61). Such humility, however, goes beyond the Augustinian type because it has its root in justification by faith alone. True humility comes only when one knows that salvation is utterly beyond one's own powers, devices, endeavors, will, and works. It depends entirely on the choice, will, and work of another, namely, of God alone. Humility, that is, is rooted in the *sola gratia*. "[W]hen a man has no doubt that everything depends on the will of God, then he completely despairs of himself and chooses nothing for himself, but waits for God to work; then he has come close to grace, and can be saved" (LW 33:62).

Why should these offensive words be published? Remember Erasmus maintained that they should not be published because he feared they would undermine human striving for virtue. But Luther saw otherwise. Virtue established on human striving does not impress God. The word on humility is to be spoken for the sake of the elect, to make and keep them humble so they can be saved. One cannot put on humility as one would put on a fancy garment. One can be made humble only by the act of grace! So God's action alone is what makes salvation possible. It has become a fashion in churchly circles these days to disparage the teaching of such despair. But Luther has some words that fit directly into the modern temper:

> It is thus for the sake of the elect that these things are published, in order that being humbled and brought back to nothingness by this means they may be saved. The rest resist this humiliation, indeed they condemn this teaching of self-despair wishing for something, however little, to be left for them to do themselves; so they remain secretly proud and enemies of the grace of God. This I say is one reason, namely, that the godly, being humbled, may recognize, call upon and receive the grace of God. (LW 33:62)

The second reason why these things should be preached comes to light in Luther's famous and perplexing statement about the very nature of faith itself. Faith, Luther insists, has to do with things not seen. In order that there be room for faith, therefore, it is necessary that everything that is to be believed should be hidden. And the deepest form of hiddenness is when it is hidden under its opposite. We have already encountered the doctrine that hiddenness is a revealed truth, not a deduction from observation. If it were the result of our observation we would take it under our control and water God down according to our ideas of what God ought to be. Here the doctrine is expanded into the understanding of a revelation under the form of opposites. That which is hidden cannot be hidden more deeply than under the form of its opposite. Thus when God makes alive he does so by killing, when he justifies he does so by making us guilty, when he exalts to heaven he does so by bringing down to hell, and so on. So, Luther says, the Scripture speaks: "The Lord kills and brings to life, He brings down to Sheol and raises up (1 Sam: 2[:6])."

Humility is not highly regarded in contemporary church and public life. But when it is rejected and God is remodeled to fit human devices the result is the loss of Christian freedom. Here the argument takes a devastating turn. Suddenly it is the very Luther who insists upon the bondage of the will who now becomes the champion of freedom! That is inevitable, of course, since a thinker like Erasmus has such a heavy investment in moral reform. Such reformers will usually end by suspecting the gospel to be the cause of immorality and by proposing various types of law as a remedy (for example, the "third use"). Luther's penetrating analysis of Erasmus' remarks about private confession is a good example of how the argument goes. Erasmus admitted that there was little or no support for private confession in either Scripture or the Fathers. Yet he suggested that it was better to keep such practices because they help to keep people moral! Luther was livid at such a procedure. "Is that the way to teach theology," he thundered, "to bind souls by laws and, as Ezekiel says [Ezek. 13:18f.], to slay them, when they are not bound by God?" This manner of "teaching theology" brings down upon us "the whole tyranny of Papal laws" (LW 33:49).

Here we see clearly that the argument takes a flip-flop. Luther is finally the champion of freedom in the debate! The moralist cannot, will not, give up. The blame for immorality must be attributed to the gospel! The "average lay person" cannot be trusted with freedom. Such thinking Luther referred to as part of the "temporal leprosy" that has to be borne, as he put it to Erasmus.

As to your fear that many who are inclined to wickedness will abuse this freedom, this should be reckoned as one of the said tumults, part of that temporal leprosy that has to be endured and that evil which has to be borne. Such people should not be considered so important that in order to prevent their abusing it the Word of God must be taken away. If all cannot be saved, yet some are saved and it is for their sake the Word of God comes. These love the more fervently and are the more inviolably in concord. For what evil did ungodly men not do even before, when there was no Word? Or rather what good did they do? . . . But now the coming of the gospel begins to be blamed for the fact that the world is wicked, whereas the truth is that the good light of the gospel reveals how the world was when it lived in its own dark-ness without the gospel. In a similar way the uneducated find fault with education because their ignorance is shown up where education flourishes. That is the gratitude we show for the Word of life and sal-vation. (LW 33:55)

In other words, why blame the gospel for the wickedness and immo-rality of the world? The failure of such theological thinking and method is evident: If one starts from the premise and defense of freedom of the will one will end in bondage. The gouty foot laughs at such doctoring. If one starts from the premise of bondage and hears the Word and prom-ise of the gospel of Christ Jesus, salvation breaks, for bondage shall be broken. But what is the nature of such bondage? The answer lies in the argument about our willing.

To sum up the argument in this "one-half of the Christian summa": God rules all things by immutable necessity. The words are harsh and difficult to take, but no amount of theological doctoring can erase or change the matter. The "God disease," if we can refer to it this way, is like the gout. It just does not go away. Another apt image Luther uses is that of the "arrow of conscience" stuck fast in the heart. I heard a rabbi in one of the memorial ceremonies for the destruction of the two World Trade Towers declaim that nothing or no one could convince us that God somehow willed the terrible tragedy with all its attendant suffering and loss of life. But the problem is that such declamations, alas, do not hold. When all is said and done, the pain and sorrow and mourning continue. The cry goes up nevertheless, *Why?* As Luther could put it, "The arrow of conviction remains stuck fast in the human heart" (Packer, 218). All such declamations accomplish is to throttle the preaching of the gospel. They substitute lame explanations and shallow comfort where there should be proclamation.

The only solution to this kind of necessity is the proclamation. That is, if God rules all things by absolute necessity, then our only recourse is to attend to what he does do. The solution to the problem of the absolute is absolution! There the immutable God does "what is necessary"! God is "determined" to have us back! But we can see that only in Christ Jesus.

Apart from Jesus we are on our own. Luther could even say that apart from Jesus God is indistinguishable from the devil. And apart from Jesus we have to attempt to redo God more to our liking or do what most moderns do, dispense with him altogether. But the gouty foot laughs at such doctoring.

# Chapter Three

# The Argument about Our Willing

*Scripture, however, represents man as one who is not only bound, wretched, captive, sick, and dead, but in addition to his other miseries is afflicted, through the agency of Satan his prince, with this misery of blindness, so that he believes himself to be free, happy, unfettered, well and alive.*

LW 33:130

This chapter is about something that really does not exist, at least not according to Martin Luther: a free will. Luther insisted against all comers that free will is a mere title, an empty name, with no reality. This was one of the main reasons for his condemnation by Rome. Luther's assertion is of course puzzling and offensive. Few things in the modern world are so cherished and fought for among us as what we call free will or free choice. It is no wonder, therefore, that Luther locked horns with Erasmus on the issue. The argument about our willing becomes, consequently, a principal indicator of Luther's understanding of what used to be called "the doctrine of man." There isn't really any good substitute for that in today's politically correct jargon, so now we have to make do with substitutes like "the doctrine of humankind" that are theologically inaccurate. The point here is that this chapter has to do with the relation and effectiveness of the human will over against the God of whom we have been speaking in the previous chapter.

What is the argument about? On the surface of it, the problem can be stated quite simply and logically. If God rules all things by absolute necessity, what ability or freedom does the creature possess to do anything at all on its own either to gain rewards or make to just retribution for misdeeds? The problem turns out to be the same as we encountered in the previous chapter. But there it was discussed largely in terms of the divine power. Here we look at it from the angle of human ability and power.

If God indeed controls all things by divine necessity, from the human perspective determinism raises its ugly and threatening countenance. Luther is often accused as a matter of course of being a "determinist." Either that, or Luther's would-be interpreters seek some way to apologize for Luther's supposed ineptitude as a systematician. So what Luther has to say will be rendered harmless. The claim will be made, for instance, that his concern is basically "religious" and not speculative or metaphysical or some such nonsense.

One wonders what Luther would say to the charge that he is a determinist. I expect that first he would reply, "Who is Luther?" That Luther may or may not be a determinist is irrelevant. The question is, "Is God?" And how shall we cope with that? Are we safe from the threat of determinism by blaming it on Luther? That is the kind of theological folly this work is intended to expose! Are we perhaps puppets, being jerked around against our wills by a malevolent puppeteer? Luther would no doubt simply hold out his arms and say, "Look, no strings." Pragmatic fact displaces useless theological speculation. Shall we save ourselves by changing the subject of the sentence from us to God? Again, the gouty foot laughs at such doctoring!

But how shall we deal with this problem? Determinism seems to bother a lot of people. And it is, of course, people who believe in God seriously who can be most troubled. Must we not use the language of will and free choice? Is it not so firmly embedded in the language that we would be rendered virtually speechless in our speaking about human activity and morals without it? Again, as Isaac Singer cleverly put it, "We

must believe in free will, we have no choice!" Luther does in fact some-
what grudgingly admit to careful use of the language of willing. And he
certainly uses it himself in his own writing and speaking. But his use of
the language of willing seems to be a restricted one, restricted, we might
say, to everyday use and communication but forbidden, or better yet, impossible with reference to God.

The instance where this is proposed most clearly is in the well-
known passage in which he makes a distinction between what is be- *Things*
neath us and what is above us. If we must use the language of free choice *above*
at all (and in Luther's view it would altogether be better not to!) we *below*
should use it with regard to those things that are beneath us but not with
regard to those things above us (LW 33:139).

How are we to understand this? Luther explains it by invoking his
customary commonsense argument. You can do what you want in the
ordinary affairs of life, that is, in that over which you really have control.
As a graffito I once saw on a college library wall put it, "All you need to
know to be free is that nothing is stopping you!" Or, to use Luther's own
words, "That is to say, a man should know that with regard to his facul-
ties and possessions he has the right to use, to do or to leave [what is beneath him] undone, according to his own free choice" (LW 33:70). To be
sure, Luther adds the remark that even such action of "free choice" is
controlled by God alone. We shall have to say more about that later. For
now the point is that in the area "beneath" we do pretty much as we
please, and God does not "interfere" even if he controls all things. We
might, of course, and we most often do, call God to account for tragedy,
failure, and disaster. But when we do we are already invading the terri-
tory of what is above us. The point here is that we are willing beings, rel-
atively successful in "doing as we please."

So we go about our normal business, making our choices without
worrying overmuch about God. We decide what clothes to wear, what
to eat, what entertainment to seek, what education to pursue, and so on.
It can even be said, I believe, that one may "decide for Jesus" if that is
found alluring. Many have done so after a fashion. Gandhi, for one, and
countless others find Jesus a fine moral and spiritual example and so on
and so on. Whether that Jesus is the Christ of God remains, of course, a

question. The Scriptures remind us that this is not to be taken for granted.

When we come to that which is above, however, we come up against something we really cannot do, or perhaps better, something we will not do, something that is truly above us. That something is, of course, a someone: Almighty God. We come up against someone to whom all the attributes of divine majesty are ascribed, who is almighty, immutable, impassible, omniscient, omnipresent, and all the other "omni" words. And when we add to the list the claims about predestination and election, we are in even bigger trouble. For the fact is that we simply cannot accept an almighty God. We cannot handle the idea of someone "above us" who we fear is controlling our destiny. When we come up against Almighty God we are bound, bound to say *no*. Be it much or be it little, we must claim at least *some freedom* to control our destiny.

So now at last, the word has entered the conversation where it belongs. We are *bound* to say no and that is precisely our bondage! Students, albeit unwittingly, often hit the nail on the head. "I can accept," they will say, "all that business about the gospel and justification by faith and so on. But I just can't buy the idea of election and predestination!" To which, of course, the only appropriate answer is, "You are absolutely right, of course! You can't buy it! That is what this whole debate is about. You have not nullified the argument, you have established it! You are bound to say no. You can't escape. Everyone theologizes as he must!" I must say to God, "God, I must have some say about my eternal destiny. You can have your necessity and your omnipotence and all of that, but when it comes to my destiny I must have at least that 'little bit' of freedom that seals the eventual outcome. You can rule the world, but I will take care of my own fate, thank you very much!"

Now here we gain decisive insight into the nature of the will's bondage. It is our reaction to the God-ness of God, our reaction to the one who is above us. The will, if there is such a thing, is captive, that is, *not free*, and thus it hardly qualifies as a real "thing."

The problem is not that we are pushed around by a god who determines all things. Determinism never really changes anything, nor does it accomplish anything. Nor does the renouncing of it, or blaming of it on

Luther, get us anywhere. As we have already seen, we do pretty much as we please in what is beneath us. You might be a libertarian and I a determinist — and after arguing about free will we decide to go and have a cup of coffee together, and nothing "metaphysical" happens. Being a determinist or a libertarian seems to make no real difference. God, apparently, does not interfere. Just how God manages to do all things by absolute necessity and still set us free is God's affair. That is a problem, Luther says, that has been in the world from the beginning and will be there at the end and though you ask much, you will never come to a satisfactory conclusion.

What is the problem? The problem is already noted in the saying about the gouty foot. The fact is that the fear of and offense at the immutable necessity of God just will not go away. The thought that a God who is supposed to be pure goodness nevertheless rules through all tragedy and suffering by absolute necessity is exceedingly offensive. Theologians and philosophers try continually to remove the offense, usually by shifting the blame from God to humans or by making distinctions in the concept of necessity, like "necessity of consequence" over against "necessity of the thing consequent." But as we have already seen, this only makes matters worse. It puts the reputed believer in the position of God, which is, of course, the essence of sin.

The prime example of this in the argument between Luther and Erasmus is the case of the hardening of Pharaoh's heart. Erasmus was mightily offended by the scriptural word which has God claiming that he would harden Pharaoh's heart in order to bring the Exodus about. Erasmus was offended, of course, because such action on God's part would negate the contribution of free will to the whole matter. Erasmus had to find some way to exonerate God and shift the blame to Pharaoh. The device Luther sees in Erasmus' argument is what they called in those days a "trope," a figure of speech. That is, the statement that God would harden Pharaoh's heart was not to be taken literally; it was really just a manner of speaking, a trope. Thus what the statement really means is that Pharaoh hardened his own heart, "as it were," when God "withdraws." To save free choice, it must be granted some "working-room." But then free choice moves in at the expense of God and his activity. God is to be simply moved off the scene. He is exonerated at the expense of his omnipotence. It would also mean that Pharaoh is ultimately in charge of the Exodus, for Pharaoh is the real actor on the stage. Luther was infuriated by this decimation of God's majesty and power as well as, eventually, God's mercy. Indeed, one could say that this kind of move by Erasmus is responsible for the demise of a serious doctrine of God in the church ever since.

It is crucial to the argument to note that the attempt to grant to free choice even the smallest place in the Exodus results in denigrating both God and man.

If grace is unconditional and free, and if one attempts to claim even the tiniest bit of merit, then everything will depend on that little bit. Grace is free. Not even a bad priest can disqualify it. What goes wrong can be charged only to that little bit. It is impossible to synthesize free grace with even the smallest bit of human cooperation. Grace becomes pernicious when it is only "a little bit." It turns back on its receiver. How much is a little bit? This is the epitome of "cheap grace," and Luther names it as such long before it became a modern shibboleth (LW 33:279).

That is why virtually the entire middle section of *The Bondage of the Will* (roughly 150 pages!) is dedicated largely to a refutation of Erasmus' and the scholastics' move to bargain away the omnipotence of God for a bit of freedom. It is, of course, an illusion. One goes only from the frying pan into the fire. There is an important theological lesson here. If you start from freedom, you will end in bondage. If you start from bondage you are more likely to end in freedom. Luther himself experienced how close he was to grace in the depths of despair: "I myself was offended more than once, and brought to the very depth and abyss of despair, so that I wished I had never been created a man, before I realized how salutary that despair was, and how near to grace" (LW 33:189).

The omnipotence of God cannot be removed by theological manipulation or rhetorical artifice. As we saw in the previous chapter, attempts to erase God's omnipotence are futile. No matter how or how much this is done, the attributes of divine majesty keep coming back. To Luther's mind they have always been so deeply implanted in the human heart and conscience that they cannot be removed. As a matter of fact

Luther here declared that we are facing up to the central issue in the whole debate.

> [T]here has always remained deeply implanted in the hearts of igno-
> rant and learned alike, whenever they have taken things seriously, the
> painful awareness that we are under necessity if the foreknowledge
> and omnipotence of God are accepted. Even natural reason herself,
> who is offended by this necessity and makes such efforts to get rid of
> it, is compelled to admit it by the force of her own judgment, even if
> there were no scripture at all. (LW 33:190)

Packer and Johnston translate the Latin a bit more dramatically and, I think, are more true to Luther: "The arrow of conviction has remained, fastened deep in the hearts of the learned and unlearned alike..." (Packer, 218). Luther repeats the same thought a bit later in dealing with the problem of how an act can be done in apparent freedom and contingency and at the same time happen under absolute divine foreknowledge.

> For it was not expected of Erasmus that he should solve the problem
> of how God can foreknow with certainty and yet things can happen
> contingently as far as we are concerned. This difficulty was in the
> world long before Diatribe. It was expected, however, that he should
> make some reply and give some definition. But instead, by availing
> himself of a rhetorical transition, he drags those of us who know no
> rhetoric away with him, as if the matters at issue here were of no mo-
> ment, but simply a lot of quibbling, and dashes bravely out of the
> crowded court crowned with ivy and laurel.
>
> But not so brother! No rhetoric has force enough to deceive an
> honest conscience; the sting of conscience. The sting of conscience is
> stronger than all the powers and resources of eloquence. We shall not
> allow a rhetorician to change the subject and confuse the issue here.
> This is not the place for that kind of trick. (LW 33:193-94)

"The turning point of the whole discussion and the very heart of the matter is in question here. And here either free choice is extinguished or it will triumph all along the line" (LW 33:194). Clearly the point is most serious for Luther. It is a matter of conscience deeply embedded in the heart. Packer and Johnston do the matter most justice with their use of the image of the arrow stuck fast in the heart. No one can pull it. Attempts to make distinctions in flights of rhetorical fancy will not stay in place. The omnipotence and immutability simply will not go away. The image of the "sting of conscience" used by the translators of the American edition is much too timid. This is a statement about the human predicament. We are beleaguered even by God and there is no escape. We are in bondage.

Here the question always arises whether this is a species of "natural theology." To be sure, Luther does say, as above, that even natural reason is forced to admit the argument. But there are some conditions that must be noted. Luther's argument about God's omnipotence and human bondage holds whenever persons take it seriously enough to be compelled to protect themselves from this God. That could happen even if no Scripture existed at all. This situation, Luther says, is the reason why so much effort has been expended to get rid of omnipotence, necessity, immutability, and the rest of the omni's. Yet it would appear that Luther does not hold strictly to a natural law view that attempts to mute the realities of God's omnipotence and human bondage. The situation in which we find ourselves before God is one which we "see" and admit to only from the point of view of being released from bondage. As the epigraph for this chapter has it, not only are we blind, but we think we can see! And that is the worst possible situation.

To move toward a summary statement of the human predicament, the root assertion on bondage is that we do not have to do with force. We are not dragged by the scruff of the neck into doing something we really do not want to do. That is what we begin to see when the light of the gospel dawns. We do what we want. And that is just the trouble! We are bound to do what we want. That is why there is no such thing, really, as a free will. Erasmus, together with those who champion free choice, makes the mistake of thinking there is a kind of neutral faculty in humans that can be turned this way or that "at will" like the neutral gear in an automobile just idling and waiting for the "driver" to make a "free decision." If one translates the matter into the language of love one begins to see more clearly how ridiculous the positing of "free will" really is. It is as if the lover should say to the beloved, "I am basically neutral about you, dear, but I have decided to consult my will in this affair and take up the option you present." One wonders what such talk would inspire!

A will is not a neutral "thing" to be turned this way and that. Such an idea is, Luther maintains, a mere logical fancy. The idea that there is in us a middle term, willing as such, to which one could affix adjectives, comes from preoccupation with words rather than the things in themselves (Packer, 115). We are, indeed, willing beings. But the point is that we are not free. A will is always willing and cannot stop. Indeed, God will not let us stop. And unless the Spirit of God enters into the matter, the will goes badly. Indeed, to attribute a "free" will to humans is not just a logical mistake, it is ultimately blasphemy (Packer, 105). For God is the only one who could be said to have free will. It is a divine name. It does not exist among humans, for they are creatures. Luther always insisted that free will was a *res de solo titulo,* a mere title only which does not exist in what we like to call "the real world."

To argue for a free will would, to borrow from the language of love again, be to argue that there is in us a "free love thing" or faculty which could be neutral or unattached. But there is no such thing as free love. Love, to be love, is always committed. That is what being in love means. The three "theological virtues" of faith, hope, and love are never neutral. If they were, they would not be what they are. Thus a will that is free is a blank space, a *no-thing,* a title without a referent, an oxymoron. Luther's argument, however, roots not so much in the logic of the will and its lack of freedom but ultimately in soteriology. Thus as the quotation at the outset of this chapter puts it, Scripture sets before us a person who is not only blind but who thinks he or she can see. The will will never be convinced of its own bondage. So the argument proceeds as a conclusion from the facts of salvation. If it is proved that our salvation is dependent on the working of God alone, then it follows that when God is not present in us to work the good then we do evil of necessity (LW 33:64).

Nevertheless Luther insists that even though we act as we do of necessity it is not a matter of being forced to act under compulsion. The presence or absence of the Holy Spirit holds the key. Luther explains:

> Now by "necessarily" I do not mean "compulsorily," but by the necessity of immutability (as they say) and not of compulsion. That is to say, when man is without the Spirit of God he does not do evil against his will, as if he were taken by the scruff of the neck and forced to do it, like a thief or robber carried off against his will to punishment, but he does it of his own accord and with a ready will. And this readiness or will to act he cannot by his own powers omit, restrain, or change, but he keeps on willing and being ready, and even if he is compelled by external force to do something different yet the will within him remains averse and he is resentful at what even compels or resists it. He would not be resentful, however, if it were changed and he willingly submitted to the compulsion. This is what we call the necessity of immutability. It means that the will cannot change itself and turn in a different direction but is rather the more provoked into willing by being resisted, as its resentment shows. This would not happen if it were free or had free choice. Ask experience how impossible it is to persuade people who have set their heart on anything. If they yield, they yield to force or to the greater attraction of something else, they never yield freely. On the other hand, if they are not set on anything they simply let things take their course. (LW 33:64-65)

The passage shows Luther's view of human willing. We are under necessity but not forced. We are not puppets controlled by a transcendent puppeteer, yet the will cannot change itself. It goes on willing what it wills and will not change because it wills immutably. It cannot change by itself because it does not want to. It is afflicted by a necessity of immutability, a not-wanting, a refusal to change. It will change externally only when it is forced to and this shows up in resentment. Or it may appear to change when attracted by something more enticing, in which case it still does not will freely but is still under immutability.

To grasp something of Luther's meaning, we should return to what he has said about our bondage in that which is above us. When we come up against the almighty God "above us," who rules all things by necessity, we are bound to say no. And we cannot, and will not, change. The problem is not that we are forced but that we do not want to. We are "bound and determined," as we often say, to have our own will. What does that mean in this case? Actually the whole argument of *The Bondage of the Will* establishes the case. No matter how much argument and demonstration or protest there may be, "the will" will go on adamantly insisting on its freedom, and doing so in blissful ignorance. Such bondage, willing, and ignorance all rolled into one is, as Luther insists, original sin itself: "Original sin itself, therefore, leaves free choice with no capacity to do anything but sin and be damned" (LW 33:272). We are not forced, but bound, actually bound!

But on the other hand Luther insists that even though bound, the will can be changed. One must note carefully what is being said when we move into such talk. Above all it is clear that God the Holy Spirit is the agent of change, not the sinner or, for that matter, the believer. "Heaven was not made for Geese," Luther quipped (LW 33:67). Thus he maintains that instead of a free will (if we must use the term), we should speak of a "vertible" or a "mutable" will, a will that can be changed. But such changing is not in the will's power of itself, "since everything depends upon the power and operation of the Holy Spirit" (LW 33:154). The reader must always bear in mind that the will is not a thing, not a faculty or some such, but something like loving and being loved, a state of being grasped, a possibility of being captivated. Thus Luther could say that he certainly acknowledged the existence of this fitness, or "dispositional quality" and "passive aptitude." Human beings, even though they cannot change themselves, can be "gotten at."

[I]f we meant by "the power of free-will" the power which makes human beings fit subjects to be caught up by the Spirit and touched by God's grace, as creatures made for eternal life or eternal death, we should have a proper definition. (Packer, 105)

The fact that the bound will is nevertheless convertible is not an opening into which Pelagius may leap with glee. The definition holds the line. God is always the actor. The discussion takes place in the context of the argument about Erasmus' attempt to rescue a "little bit" of power for the will, to give free choice a role to play and keep things under control. But it cannot work. As we have established repeatedly it is impossible to mix a little human willpower with the divine in order to make room for morality and freedom. If salvation is reputedly given entirely by grace and one tries to work in a little bit of "free choice" then everything, absolutely everything, will depend on that little bit. It cannot escape being salvation by works alone.

This also, as we noted earlier, is the real root of "cheap grace," for it proposes that one can have grace at "bargain basement" prices. Luther was on to that game way back in Reformation times (Packer, 268-69). It was for this reason that Luther believed that semi-Pelagians are much worse than full-blooded Pelagians, because Pelagians hold that God's grace cannot be purchased for a pittance — at least they put their whole heart in the matter. God's grace is made cheap by semi-Pelagians precisely by attempting to raise the price ever so slightly!

But when the Spirit of God enters the picture everything changes. The will, which we have seen is convertible, is really changed. We are indeed still under the "sweet influence" of the Spirit of God. We are indeed still bound, but now bound by the Spirit in such fashion that we cannot be "overcome or compelled even by the gates of hell" (LW 33:64). The battle is now drawn. The believer begins to see what original sin actually is. A new freedom dawns which Luther called the royal freedom. The will does spontaneously what the Spirit "inspires." The "Stronger One" has invaded the house and cast out the strong man armed. Thus we are taken as the spoil of the stronger one and held gladly as his captives. Freedom and spontaneity is the happy result (LW 33:65).

This, incidentally, is the setting for Luther's infamous interpretation of the beast with two riders. It is perhaps the best-known passage from *The Bondage of the Will,* and the most quoted, though seldom without a shudder. Luther likens the human will to a beast between two riders. If Satan rides, it goes where Satan wills. If God rides, it goes and wills to go where God wills. In either case there is no "free choice." It is rather a matter of being taken captive, of being captivated, finally, by the Spirit of God. Thus Luther says, "But if a Stronger one comes who overcomes [Satan] and takes us as his spoil, then through his Spirit we are again slaves and captives — though this is royal freedom" (LW 33:65).

Dismay over Luther's use of the image is due on the one hand to failure to gauge carefully the context in which it is set, and on the other of course to the antipathy to the doctrine of bondage itself. Luther intends with the image to set forth as passionately and intently as possible the spontaneity of the relation between God the Spirit and the redeemed. The entry of the Spirit into one's life is not a polite choice but a radical change, something more like an invasion, a breaking into the house of the "strong man armed," a move, or rather a being moved, from death to life. This brings us to the argument about soteriology, Christ's work in salvation.

*Chapter Four*

# The Argument about Christ and Salvation

*Moreover, since Christ is said to be "the way, the truth, and the life" (John 14:6), and that categorically, so that whatever is not Christ is not the way, but error, not truth, but untruth, not life, but death, it follows of necessity that "free will," inasmuch as it neither is Christ, nor is in Christ, is fast bound in error, and untruth and death. Where and whence, then, comes your intermediate, neutral entity (I mean the power of "free will") which, though it is not Christ (that is, the way, the truth and the life), should not be error, or untruth, or death? If all the things that are said of Christ and of grace were not said categorically, so that they may be contrasted with their opposites, like this: out of Christ there is nothing but Satan, out of grace nothing but wrath, out of light nothing but darkness, out of the way nothing but error, out of the truth nothing but a lie, out of life nothing but death — were these things not so, what, I ask you would be the use of all the apostolic discourses and, indeed, of the entire Scriptures? They would all be written in vain, for they would not compel the admission that men need Christ (which is their main burden), and that for the following reason: something intermediate would be found which, of itself, would be neither evil nor good, neither Christ's nor Satan's, neither true nor false, neither alive nor dead, neither something nor nothing (perhaps), and its*

61

*name would be called "the most excellent and exalted thing in the whole human race"!*

(Packer, 307)

Lurking behind the argument about free will is, of course, the question of salvation. In the Erasmian way of thinking there can be in effect no salvation unless there is free will. How else could one appropriate grace? How could one respond to the biblical commands and mandates? Unable to grasp what Luther had been saying, Erasmus cries out virtually in exasperation:

> What can be more useless than to publish to the world the paradox that all we do is done, not by "free will," but of mere necessity, and Augustine's view that God works in us both good and evil; that he rewards his own good works in us, and punishes his own evil works in us? What a flood-gate of iniquity would the spread of such news open to people! What wicked man would amend his life? Who would believe that God loved him? Who would fight against his flesh? (Packer, 97)

One cannot help but note the basic moralism of the Erasmian position. That is the nature of the case. Freedom of choice in matters "above us" issues inevitably and irrevocably in moralism. Indeed, from the point of view espoused by Erasmus nothing could be more useless than to publish abroad the "paradoxes" that God works all things by his immutable necessity, including good and evil in us. If the common herd gets wind of that, who will be good? Amendment of life, doing good, stopping that notorious "flood-gate" of evil that Erasmus so desperately fears — all have a prime place in the soteriology of free will. Moralism is its understanding of salvation.

But Luther forges adamantly ahead. If these paradoxes were of men there would be little point in getting worked up about them. But since they come to us as the Word of God from Holy Scripture it is a different matter altogether. The paradoxes of Scripture drive home to us the weight of the marvel of salvation. Everything, just everything, must be shut down so that God alone in the power of the Holy Spirit shall be the savior from the moralism proposed. The Erasmian view is what destroys us.

So Luther sails into the storm and takes up Erasmus' questions: Who will try and reform his life? Who will believe that God loves him? What of that "flood-gate of iniquity" supposedly unleashed by the idea that God works evil and good in us? And so forth. Luther replies with a steadfast and crushing *nobody, nobody can!* "God has no time for your practitioners of self-reformation, for they are hypocrites" (Packer, 99). God, that is, is simply not interested in a self-made righteousness. He is not interested in a righteousness manufactured out of the stuff of free will. Who then will believe? Nobody! But then will not the floodgate of iniquity be unleashed upon us? So be it! It is surely the utmost folly to think that if God has sent evil to plague us free will is going to stop it!

But there is a positive side to these negative assertions. Those who seek their salvation in the constructions of free choice, that is, by constructing a theology amenable to free choice, shall perish unreformed. But the elect, who fear God, will be reformed by the Holy Spirit. The positive side to the question and the final "solution" comes in the doctrine of election. Election is the breaking through into the present of the divine word of promise. The words we have just heard, the resounding *no* and *nobody can,* are, Luther insists, "the very doctrines which throw open to the elect who fear God a gateway to righteousness, an entrance into heaven, and a road to God!" (Packer, 99).

How so? The best way to understand Luther here is to recall what he has said in various forms repeatedly. Near the end of his life Luther took up a series of lectures on the book of Genesis. In the twenty-sixth chapter he set about answering the charge that election and predestination made human action pointless. Luther had heard that among nobles and "persons of importance" the argument went like this: "If I am elect I shall go to heaven or hell regardless of what I do!" Luther responded by insisting that this reaction to God's election is original sin itself (LW 5:42). It is not often appreciated what such a response entails. It is not simply that the words of a question like that are mistaken, as if the theologian only failed to put them together in the proper order and so on, but that the very presumption of that theological conclusion in the face of God's true hiddenness is mistaken. The attempt to make God answerable to the likes of us — that is the original sin itself. Small wonder that Luther here, as elsewhere, moves to a full discussion of the hiddenness of God in order to respond. Moralists and amoralists are in the same predicament before the divine majesty, and do not know what to do — so they plow ahead by denying the divine majesty and blaspheme God:

> Now that we have actually come, not just to the doctrines of scripture
> . . but to the awful secret of God's Majesty — that is, as was said, the
> question why does He work as He does — here you break down the
> barriers and burst in all but blaspheming! What indignation against
> God do you not display because you may not see the reason and de-
> sign of his counsel!" (Packer, 99)

That is the key to the matter: indignation against God! Once again the gouty foot laughs at such doctoring! The pain simply will not go away. Erasmus thinks he is constructing an apologetic that will make God more believable, but he is only bringing theology to the edge of despair and blasphemy — if not pushing it into Bunyan's slough of despond all together! The point is that God simply refuses to be known in his "naked majesty." That is both good news and bad news — good news because no one can see God and live (better in that case that God hide!); bad news because no one can see God. God graciously hides from sinners and so we are bound to a fruitless search for God or a desperate flight from him.

The Erasmian apologetic simply makes matters worse. Luther sees this clearly and sets it forth in his inimitable, sarcastic fashion. He sees clearly that his own position is an attack on the God of classical antiquity, especially Aristotle's "unmoved mover."

> Aristotle also depicts for us a God of this kind, that is, one who is
> asleep, and who leaves it for anyone to use or abuse His long-

suffering and chastisement at will. Nor can reason come to any other conclusion about God than the Diatribe does here. As she herself snores over and makes light of the things of God, so she thinks of God as snoring over them too, not using His wisdom, will and presence to elect, separate and inspire, but entrusting to men the tiresome business of heeding or defying His long-suffering and anger! This is what we come to when we seek to measure God and make excuses for Him by human reason, not reverencing the secrets of his majesty, but peering and probing into them; with the result that we are overwhelmed by the glory of them and instead of a single excuse we vomit a thousand blasphemies! We forget ourselves and gabble like lunatics, speaking against both God and ourselves, while all the time we were intending, in the greatness of our wisdom, to plead both God's cause and our own! (Packer, 200)

Particularly to be noted is the fact that the apologetic of one like Erasmus ends by "speaking against both God and ourselves." In other words the apologetic backfires! How so? We have encountered this several times in the course of the argument. When free and unconditional grace is tempered by a "little bit" of free-will theology, the sinner is left to himself or herself to find the way. Since grace is free the fault for all misdoing falls on the sinner. The good news turns inexorably on the sinner and his or her free will. God, likewise, is robbed of his power as the savior and elector. If Erasmus is right, Luther maintains, God will elect no one and the world will be left to its own devices. Soon one arrives at the picture of a God who does nothing to save us! Aristotle's God! One ends by "gabbling like lunatics," speaking against both God and ourselves, thinking in the greatness of our wisdom to plead both God's cause and our own! The free will apologetic only makes matters worse.

This, by the way, is also Luther's judgment on Pelagianism, Semi-Pelagianism, and all forms of synergism. Any attempt to make a synthesis between God's unconditional grace and human effort ends by cheapening grace. This is the real source of complaints about cheap grace. A full-blown Pelagianism, he always maintained, is better than a Semi-Pelagianism. A full-blown Pelagianism will at least insist that one has to exert full strength to gain salvation whereas a Semi-Pelagian exerts only a partial effort — a kind of "bargain basement" salvation! This is real cheap grace and the devil's playground. "Apart from grace, 'free-will' by itself is Satan's kingdom in all men" (Packer, 201).

But the question for this chapter is how can soteriology "work"? If God rules all things by necessity and the prospective believer appears as an offended and confused "puppet," how shall the saving work of Christ proceed? Erasmus, together with virtually the whole modern world, found Luther's acceptance of the scriptural account of such matters as the hardening of Pharaoh's heart, or that a just and good God would require impossibilities, or the laying of sin onto the free will even though it is driven by necessity, simply horrendous. In other words we find ourselves confronted squarely with the problem of evil.

Again we find ourselves at a parting of the ways. The free-will theologian like Erasmus finds all these things absurd and takes the road of constructing an apology or redoing divinity in terms more acceptable to "reason." So he employs similes, tropes, or other figures of speech to interpret his way out of trouble. So, good and evil can be likened to good and bad clay, for example. The sun shines on both and one is hardened while the other is melted away. The fault therefore is not God's but the evil in the bad clay and so on. Luther was not impressed by such exegetical nonsense. It lands one in a worse position than before. To "save God" we end with a Gnostic-type dualism of two different kinds of being: good clay and bad! With that assumption, whatever freedom there was is gone and God is simply erased as a significant actor in the drama.

Erasmus appealed once again to his idea that Paul should be preached according to the wisdom of the hearers, adapted, that is, to the level of the hearers' ability. In that way, it is to be assumed that the dreadful news of election will not fall on ignorant ears. But, as we have already seen, Luther would have none of this sort of attempt to hide the message from "the common herd," as Erasmus was wont to call common folk. "Silly ignorant remarks," he says of Erasmus' whole preface to the *Diatribe*. We teach nothing save Christ and him crucified. "But Christ crucified brings all these doctrines with him including wisdom also among them that are perfect" (Packer, 107-8). Luther will brook no foolery at this point. Not exegetical manipulation, tropological or symbolic evasion of issues, attempts to limit their authority to "the wise" — in short, any and all the exegetical tricks in the bag. None of it can be allowed. Something new is breaking in.

But how shall salvation proceed if there is no possibility of free choice? This above all infuriated Erasmus as it continues to infuriate his champions down to the present day. If God rules all things by necessity how can there be any sincere appropriation of the grace of God, any merit in doing justice, any obedience to the divine will announced in Scripture, and so on? How can the believer be anything but a puppet? In short, how can there be any genuine faith, repentance, or devotion? It seems as if the believer is cut out of the act of salvation itself!

Of course this has been the problem all along. It is the constant problem hurled at anyone or any "system" that takes grace alone seriously. "But does grace alone not lead to ethical quietism and moral laxity?" So the question goes and will go until the end of time. Thinkers like Erasmus, whose predominant aim is moral reform, can never seem to avoid the trap. Luther called it the presumption of law. Law always nags and drives. We cannot (will not!) escape it. That is why we need the Holy Spirit to break its hold. That is the work, indeed the essential work, of soteriology.

To that we turn now. The solution to "the problem" posed by the bondage of the will is preaching. How can we be sure that God is out to save us? The matter is really quite simple. It is because God rules all things by necessity and will not change his mind. That may cause us some difficulty when we come to questions raised by the likes of Erasmus but we can address them later. For now we turn to look at the place and point of preaching. When I say preaching I believe one must encompass the entire office of the ministry of the church including the sacraments as well as the more formal act of "declaring the word" in liturgy, song, confession, and so on.

The point of preaching is that it is the instance in which the God who rules all things by necessity reveals what it is that he necessarily wills. The preacher, that is, has the authority from the Lord Jesus actually to do the electing! This is usually astounding news to most Christians and unfortunately to too many preachers. The result is that instead of preaching or proclaiming, the church ends up telling stories or lecturing on selected religious topics. This, essentially, is to take the place of Erasmus when he declared that one should not bother the common herd with such difficult topics as divine necessity, election, predestination, and the like.

But how does Luther respond? He goes right to the heart of the matter: the preaching, the proclamation. "If God does not govern all things by his unchanging power, who will believe his promises?" (Packer, 84). So we have the strange situation in which that which was considered the cause of the problem is taken by Luther to be the solution. Here we come again to a fundamental parting of the ways! Erasmus asks how there can be faith, ethics, true piety, in short, true Christian life if God rules all things by immutable necessity. Luther maintains that faith cannot be sure of itself unless God does so rule. For then we would be in the hands of just that God from whom we are attempting to escape: fate!

But if we have to do with the preached God who makes immutable promises we have to do with someone entirely different. Without that there is no solid faith. Luther puts it in excellent fashion:

> If then, we are taught and believe that we ought to be ignorant of the necessary foreknowledge and the necessity of events, Christian faith is utterly destroyed, and the promises of God and the whole gospel fall to the ground completely, for the Christian's chief and only comfort in every adversity lies in knowing that God does not lie, but brings all things to pass immutably and that His will cannot be resisted, altered or impeded. (Packer, 84)

Imagine that! The entire gospel is destroyed if one tries like Erasmus, and most theologians still these days, to avoid the problem of necessity. Luther's words are of course frightening if one does not bear in mind that it is against the background of God not preached and God preached that such words can be spoken. We do not have to do with an abstract God of fate nor with a frozen "first principle" but with a God who makes promises and keeps them and will not surrender them. What can we do about such a God? Listen to him! The answer to our problem is in the preached God. But it cannot be forgotten that the gospel, and only the gospel, spells the end of the hidden God. More of that later. For now we need to say more about soteriology.

Erasmian soteriology spells itself out in argument over several passages that seem to support free choice. For him, passages that seem not to support free choice are, as we have seen, to be interpreted tropologically or symbolically. Free choice is the "inference," the trope by which Scripture is to be interpreted. Think on it! The entire history of God with his people is reversed. God is no longer the sole actor. Room must be reserved for the likes of Pharaoh! But what sort of savior will Pharaoh be?

The argument comes through the clearest, and issues in something of a systematic statement, in the debate over Ecclesiasticus 15:14-17: "God from the beginning made man, and left him in the hand of his own counsel. He added also his commandments and his precepts, saying, If thou art willing to keep my commandments, and to keep continually the faith that pleaseth me, they shall preserve thee. He hath set before thee fire and water; and upon which thou wilt, stretch forth thine hand. Before man is life and death; and whichever pleaseth him shall be given unto him" (Packer, 143).

To start with, Luther declares that he could with justice refuse to allow this book into the debate since it is apocryphal. But he will allow it in order to avoid unnecessary quibbling at this point about the canon. This means that Luther has a very interesting task of interpretation to face up to. Apocryphal books tend to reflect freedom of the will rather than bondage. The particular passage that attracted Erasmus is a good example. It was only natural for him to use it for his argument. Luther reads the passage in a radically different sense from Erasmus. Once again we see that we are confronted by two radically different understandings of the self and its freedom.

It is not necessary, I think, to recite Erasmus' view of the matter here once again. Nothing new is offered and for Luther it is just "shooting fish in a barrel," as the saying goes. What is new is the appearance of something like a systematic structure, which gives us clues to Luther's understanding of the matter. Throughout the treatise Erasmus has, with the entire Western tradition by and large, assumed the idea of what might be called the "downward fall." The creature, that is, was given a place of at least relative perfection in the creation.

But this means nothing but trouble for the understanding of sin and freedom. Sin is conceived as a downward plunge. The very word "fall" already indicates that. It is not, one can say, a good biblical term. For the downward fall debate always descends to the level of argument about how much freedom is lost and how much must be left to prevent one from falling off the scale of perfection altogether. Furious defenses must be constructed to prevent complete collapse. And that, of course, is what this book is about.

Erasmus tried to ameliorate the problem by claiming to find three different views of free will in the church. The first Erasmus finds is the view of those who admit that one cannot will the good without special grace, that is, cannot start, make progress, or finish the project. Erasmus is willing to accept this view, even though he thinks it "severe enough." This is the view of those who think they have satisfied the call to "grace alone" by calling it to perform the task of a helping hand to the divine free will. Humans are called to proper effort, but not such that they can claim any merit of their own. Grace is *"sola"* only in the sense that without it one can do nothing good.

The second view is that free will avails for nothing but sinning. Erasmus finds this view "more severe" and clearly wants to distance himself from such a view. The third view is the view that Erasmus wants to identify with Luther and is accorded the rank of "most severe." This is the view, Erasmus says, of those who say that free will is an empty term, and that God works in us both good and evil, and all that comes to pass is of mere necessity.

One can see, of course, the scholastic mind at work in Erasmus' move. He divides free will into three types and then chooses the one obviously most pleasing to free will. In other words, he uses free will to solve the problem of free will! Luther saw this immediately. "In a word, wherever the Diatribe turns it cannot keep clear of inconsistencies and contradictions, nor avoid making that very 'free will' which it defends as much a prisoner as itself. In trying to free the will it gets so entangled that it ends up bound itself." The entire section that follows shows clearly that the result is a kind of play on words with no real referent. For Luther the three views Erasmus propounds in the *Diatribe* are really all the same. Luther insists that he meant nothing other than the first view throughout. For to say that the will cannot will the good without grace is the same as to say that the will is not free (Packer, 144ff.).

Luther's argument is that a will to be a will must will something. Otherwise it becomes a pure verbal abstraction. He refers to it as the "dream" of the *Diatribe,* the idea that between ability to will the good or not to will the good there may be a third neutral or middle term that wills nothing, or has lost its freedom. But to will nothing or to lose its freedom is for will to be trapped in the worst kind of bondage. Thinking to save a place in the system for free will one loses it altogether.

Here one begins to see the inescapable nature of the bondage. Luther sees clearly that the claims of and for free will are due to a fatal flaw in the use of language: "It is a mere logical fancy that there is in man a middle term, *willing* as such; nor can those who assert it prove it. The notion sprang from ignorance of things and preoccupation with words: As though things always correspond in fact to the verbal analysis of them!" (Packer, 147). For Erasmus the will always seems to be that neutral gear in an automobile which can be shifted this way and that "at will." But this, Luther insists, is mere abstraction, a logical fiction. A will, to be a will, always wills something, either good or evil. "The sophist," Luther holds, "makes endless error over this."

> The truth is rather as Christ puts it: He that is not with me is against me (Matt. 12:30). He does not say: he that is not with me is not against me either, but is in an intermediate position! For if God is in us, Satan is out of us, and then it is present with us to will only good. But if God is not in us, Satan is, and then it is present with us to will only evil. Neither God nor Satan permits there to be in us mere willing in the abstract, but as you rightly said, we have lost our freedom and are

forced to serve — sin — that is, we *will* sin and evil, and *speak* sin and evil, we *do* sin and evil!" (Packer, 147, emphasis added)

But we must return to the Ecclesiasticus passage to get at the depth of the argument. And we should make no mistake about it. It is eventually all about soteriology. It is about whether the church can and will speak the saving gospel word or will only confront the hearers with death-dealing law.

The argument was about who had the right to claim the Ecclesiasticus passage for his side of the argument. It would seem at first glance that Erasmus would have the better of it. It is basically an interpretation of the fall story. Luther summarizes the essentials of the argument in his response to Erasmus. First it says that God made man at the beginning. Here it speaks of man's creation, not about human free will or commandments. It goes on to say that God left the creature in the hand of his own council (Packer, 151).

Is this the place where free will enters the scene? But look again at this first verse: "God from the beginning made man, and left him in the hand of his own counsel." There is no mention of commandments, Luther says, for the performance of which free will is required. Nothing is said about this in the discussion about creation. This is a very interesting and important reservation for Luther's understanding of law and its relation to human free will. It should be noted carefully. What does the latter half of the verse mean? Luther takes it to mean humanity's commission to exercise lordship over creation and care for it. The amazing thing is that Luther does not allow law to intrude on creation. There are no commandments standing over creation!

If anything is meant by the phrase "in the hand of his own counsel," therefore, it has to be understood along the lines of the Genesis creation account, that the human creature is to be lord of all things and have dominion according to his own will (Packer, 150). But when does the question of free will or bondage then arise? It arises, according to the Ecclesiasticus text, when we arrive at words about God "adding his own" commandments and precepts. The question then is, added them to what? Naturally it has to be to the counsel and will of man. And this can only mean, Luther avers, that we are now dealing with that which is above us. This means for Luther that God *took from* the creature his dominion over one part of the creation. What part? The tree of the knowledge of good and evil! There he willed that the creature should *not* be free.

Having reached the point where the commandments and counsels are added we come to a crucial point for the understanding of bondage. The commandments and counsels do not enhance or make freedom possible, they take it away! The usual way is to think that law and command make freedom possible. For Luther, nothing could be further from the truth. When the law strikes, death takes over. St. Paul said it: When the law came, sin revived and I died (Rom. 7:9).

When the commandments and the counsels are added we arrive at the fundamental problem of the will of the creature over against the will of the creator. The all-important issue is stated: "If thou art willing to keep my commandments and precepts, they shall preserve thee." With the posing of this question — Is the will free to do the commandments and keep the counsels? — the argument over free will proceeds. Obviously the creature is accorded freedom of some sort. This is indicated by the fact that the creator left the creature in the hand of his own counsel in this age. But the fact that the creator withdrew power over part of creation means that the creator remains God nevertheless and retains the Divine Lordship over all. The question for the creature is whether he or she will remain a creature, or rebel and attempt to take the power for the self. The rebellion may then aptly be termed a rebellion upward, the creature attempting to take the place of the creator.

Thus the structure of the rebellion is complete. It is an upward rebellion, rebellion against God and his power. The Erasmian attempt to claim the Ecclesiasticus passage for the "free will" argument without dispute, Luther believes, has been rendered questionable if not harmless. The basic structure, Luther finds, is that of the two kingdoms and the fact that free will is not granted to the creature by such passages but is rather taken away:

With the words, then, "if thou art willing," the discussion of "free will" begins. So we learn from Ecclesiasticus that man falls under two kingdoms. In the one, he is led by his own will and counsel, not by any precepts and commandments of God; that is, in the realm of things below him. Here he reigns and is lord, as being left in the hand of his own counsel. Not that God leaves him alone in the sense that He does not co-operate with him in all things; but in the sense that He has granted him a free use of things at his own will, and not hedged him in with any laws or commands. You could say by way of parallel that the Gospel has left us in the hand of our own counsel, to use and have dominion over things as we will; whereas Moses and the Pope did not leave us to that counsel, but constrained us by laws and subjected us rather to their will. In the other kingdom, however, man is not left in the hand of his own counsel, but directed and led by the will and counsel of God. As in his own kingdom he is led by his own will and not by the precepts of another, so in the kingdom of God he is led by the precepts of another, and not by his own will. This is what Ecclesiasticus means when he says: "he added also his commandments and his precepts, saying, 'If thou are willing,'" etc. (Packer, 150-51).

Why did Luther enter into this rather complicated argument? Because Erasmus believed, no doubt, that here was one of the clearest and most direct statements of free choice in Scripture. Even though it was not canonical it was hard to escape. Erasmus is a clear proponent of the "downward fall." But with the "two kingdoms" doctrine Luther took on the charge to demonstrate that the passage is best interpreted in accordance with the proper biblical understanding of bondage of the will. So he concludes by gleefully announcing his victory. What he has done, as a matter of fact, is to show that the passages in question can be, indeed must be, interpreted in terms of the universal biblical understanding — that is, one that uses a proper biblical understanding of the fall rather than Erasmus' inference of a "downward fall." Even this extra-canonical passage, Luther concluded, therefore could not unambiguously be used to establish the argument for free choice. Of course humans enjoy a certain degree of freedom. But it is freedom that belongs and operates in the kingdom "on the left." The distinction between two kingdoms is vital for a proper grasp of the gospel.

The Ecclesiasticus passage was only the beginning, however, of a lengthy discussion of such biblical passages in which Erasmus seeks to nail down such a general or universal biblical understanding. Erasmus argues, in effect, that he has the high ground interpreting the scriptural passages that seem to imply free choice. So Luther takes on such passages once again. It is not necessary here for us to give an exhaustive account of all the passages. As we have already pointed out in the section on Scripture, the number of passages for or against something is quite irrelevant. It will be sufficient to follow the argument in summary fashion. In this way we will solidify the final shape of the argument.

Why does God issue so many demands and commands through the Holy Scripture if the will is unable to fulfill then? Is God not simply mocking us if he places us in such a position? Luther's reply: These are the inferences of human reason which, if taken seriously, would have disastrous consequences. Throughout his argument Luther again and again attacks such inferences. In the first place he insists that Erasmus cannot follow such inferences himself if he is to remain at all true to what he has previously maintained. He has agreed that the view which is "most probable" allows that free will cannot will any good. But if that is so, how can the Ecclesiasticus statement have any meaning?

The *Diatribe*, Luther likes to point out, always gets trapped in its own inferences. It wants to infer freedom of choice from the text but the text always imposes bondage. Commandments do not grant freedom, they take it away. That is a hard but indispensable theological lesson to learn. "Reason," Luther says, "is thus so entrapped in the inferences and words of her own wisdom, that she does not know what she is saying or talking about. It is, however, entirely appropriate that free will should be defended with the sort of arguments that mutually devour and destroy one another" (Packer, 154). If one were to draw inferences properly from the Ecclesiasticus passage one would have to conclude the argument by saying, "Since we are willing therefore we are able to keep the commandments!" What appears out of the whole confusion is a Kantian "Du kanst denn du solst" (You can therefore you ought).

Luther was of course quick enough to see that Erasmus' attempt to claim freedom on the basis of the Ecclesiasticus-text view lands him squarely in the camp of the Pelagians. Luther repeatedly raises the charge of Pelagianism in his critique of Erasmus' *Diatribe,* perhaps most pointedly in the claim that Erasmus is actually less honest about works than Pelagius. How so? Because Erasmus claims that one need only a little bit of grace whereas Pelagius seeks it all. Pelagius, that is, implies that Christians should seek perfection, not just a kind of "bargain basement" possibility. The end of the argument that Erasmus is trying to make will only force a choice between half-way or full Pelagianism. One could say he is bound to it.

# Postscript

Luther recognized that Erasmus put his finger on the heart of the matter. Erasmus wanted to argue that God would not have given us all these commandments if there were no possibility of fulfilling them. Law would then be indirect proof of freedom. The problem is that such indirect, would-be schemes of salvation always lead into a trap. Inferences like Erasmus' always enslave us, especially inferences about the law. So Luther would answer Erasmus, "Hold on a minute, the law doesn't prove freedom; it takes freedom away!" Freedom is not a reward that is realized — that thinking takes us right back into the law. Such inferences always begin and end with the law for the person trying to establish the powers of the free will. Use of the law in that way is automatic and deadly. That is the bondage.

The issue is exposed when one comes up against the *deus absconditus*. Erasmus does not really know what kind of a trap he is in. The fallacy of his whole argument is that he is left to infer what God must be like merely from the law, while the Holy Spirit is out making assertions apart from the law concerning the Father's only Son, Jesus Christ. In the middle of the argument Luther breaks out in the confession, "He sent his *Son* to save us." That is the heart and soul of his entire argument. The work of theology is not for making inferences from the law, but for a proclamation that is all about Christ. It is not about human possibilities and limitations, but what the Father is doing in his Son to reconcile the world to himself. Luther simply recognized that if the Father is sending his Son to save us, it is not the law that frees.

The problem of this freedom for Erasmus is that God robs us of all our claims to work salvation by ourselves and sets about to captivate us. God's very Godness then is the problem. But for Luther, God's own way of being God is also the only solution to the conundrum of human freedom precisely because he sent his Son to save us. All other inferred or preferred solutions are bogus, and it is such bogus theology that has been cheating the church ever since.

The preaching of Jesus Christ and him crucified on account of sinners is God's desired way of being God. That means, according to Luther, that preaching must be categorical. In today's jargon that means unconditional. Proclamation that gives forgiveness to sinners on account of Christ alone is the only solution for all our problems with God. The only way to end the threat of the unpreached God is by the preached God. That is the presupposition for all Christian preaching and the reason for this book. Luther is adamant at this point:

> For if you doubt or disdain to know that God foreknows all things, not contingently, but necessarily and immutably, how can you believe his promises and place a sure trust and reliance on them? . . . For this is the one supreme consolation of Christians in all adversities, to know that God does not lie, but does all things immutably, and that his will can neither be resisted nor changed nor hindered. (LW 33:42-43)

In this way, only preaching that assumes the bondage of the will for its hearers truly comes to free. Preaching, however, seems to have gotten off the track of late. And when that is the case preaching degenerates into telling cute stories with the preacher taking over as the primary narrator. The preaching then either gives anecdotes or talks about personal experience. Instead, the kind of categorical preaching that Luther describes gives a God who is truly preached. The God whom we discover ourselves is always a hidden God, literally a God not preached. The climax of this hiddenness is that God robs us of all our claims to work salvation by ourselves. Ultimately no preachers can then remain the subjects of their own fantasies. The only way to overcome the problem of the hiddenness of God not preached is by God preached. But that will not happen by attempting to infer God's will from the law. It happens only when the preaching is categorical, unconditional, just as God did not spare his Son but gave him to captivate our bound wills, drawing all to himself.

People sometimes complain that Luther seems to know an awful lot about the hidden God. Luther would simply answer, "Christ crucified draws all these things with him." God sent his Son to save us, and instead of our discovering a hidden God it is God who discovers us. So it is that the Father says, "This is my beloved Son, listen to Him!" (Luke 9:35). God does not lie, "but does all things immutably," especially in the promise of his beloved Son, so "take the saying of Christ in John 6[:44]: 'No one comes to me unless my Father draws him.' What does this leave to free choice?" (LW 33:285). That is the heart of the matter.

# Sermons

# The Easy Yoke

*"Come to me, all who labor and are heavy laden, and I will give you rest. Take my yoke upon you, and learn from me; for I am gentle and lowly in heart, and you will find rest for your souls. For my yoke is easy, my burden is light."*

Matt. 11:28-30

In an age when the storms of criticism swirl about us, theology can become a heavy burden to bear. It seems to carry so much freight which the voices of the world tell us is just too hard to believe, and too heavy a load to carry. These voices bid us to cast off the burden, to lighten the load, to reduce it to that bare minimum which, supposedly, reasonable souls are able to carry. We all hear these voices and react to them in various ways. The trouble is that our various reactions work only to increase the abrasiveness of the task of theology and give rise to bitterness. Those who are more "conservative" can become bitter because they think that others are not carrying their share of the burden, or that they may have cast off something that is essential. Those who are more "liberal" can become bitter because they feel that their "conservative" friends are sitting in judgment and insisting that they bear a heavier burden than is right or necessary to bear. And in our relationships with one another, professor to student, and student to fellow student, we can become increasingly cynical about one another's theology and bitter about the yoke we think we are being forced to bear.

When I was thinking about this common problem of ours, I was struck by the way in which Matthew puts the two sayings of Jesus together in our text for today, the one saying about *revelation,* and the other saying about the easy *yoke.* In the first, Jesus says, "I thank thee Father . . . that thou hast hidden these things from the wise and understanding and revealed them to babes; yea, Father, for such was thy gracious will. All things have been delivered to me by my Father; and no one knows the Son except the Father; and no one knows the Father except the Son and anyone to whom the Son chooses to reveal him" (Matt. 11:26-27).

One might expect, I suppose, after a saying so pregnant with theological content as that, a discourse on the seriousness of the burden of theology, what a grave task it is, and how important it is to get everything straight. But no! These words are followed immediately by the words, "Come to me, all who labor and are heavy laden, and I will give you rest. Take my yoke upon you, and learn from me; for I am gentle and lowly in heart, and you will find rest for your souls. For my yoke is easy, my burden is light."

The fact that these two sayings are put together gives us an insight into what theology is all about. As theologians we are not, one hopes, in the business of laying heavy burdens on the world or on one another. Theology is the happy science concerned with the task of pointing to him whose yoke is easy, whose burden is light. Theology is not in the business of absolutizing itself, but rather of pointing beyond itself to the one who gives hope, the one in whom we can find rest. Theology is perhaps the only science which is ultimately and seriously interested in working itself out of a job, for it points in hope to that time when Christ will come and all theology will cease. Theology is only an interim science. It exists only because he to whom it points is not yet here. Its only task is the happy one of helping to keep hope alive until he comes.

This does not mean, however, that theology is an easy study. The fact that his yoke is easy and his burden is light is not an invitation to slovenliness or laziness. For the problem is precisely that we as human beings, as sinners, are clever and devious masters at the art of laying heavy burdens upon ourselves. Thinking to lighten the load *for ourselves* and *by ourselves* through our own theological cleverness or reductionism we more often than not succeed only in making the burden heavier. It is the real task of theology to smell out and expose this deviousness, be it conservative or liberal. And this is a hard and exacting task, calling for all the intellectual wisdom and effort that we can muster. But it is, or at least it should be, a joyful task, the joyful task of lifting the burdens under which we suffer so as to point to him whose yoke is easy, whose burden is light.

Perhaps if we could grasp this we would find that some of our bitterness would dissolve and we could all join in the common task without rancor. The common task, that is, of exposing the fraud of the burdens we lay upon ourselves and pointing to him who says to you, "Come to me, all you who labor and are heavy laden, and I will give you rest."

## *Justification by Faith Alone*

*"We hold that a man is justified by faith apart from works of law."*

Rom. 3:28

That is the word that broke in upon the world through the ministry of Martin Luther so long ago and fired the Reformation. It was a word that shocked the world then, and it still shocks and angers the world today. It shocked the world when St. Paul first preached it to the Romans. It comes to us like a bolt from the blue, like a strange comet from some unknown realm. For who has heard of such a thing — that one is made right with God just by stopping all activity, being still and listening? What the words say to us, really, is that for once in your life you must just shut up and listen to God, listen to the announcement: You are just before God for Jesus' sake!

Strange words. Indeed more and more today we find people asking, "Who needs them?" Perhaps back in Luther's day, we are told, when people were really trying to save themselves by doing good works, justification by faith was good news. But who is trying anymore? In the day of the Reformation a person suffered from an anxious conscience, but is that true anymore? It seems that we have this marvelous cure, but no one has the disease! So we stand, as Luther often said, like a cow staring at a new gate, wondering what these words have to do with us. Is there not something much more relevant to say?

But before we go any farther we have to pause and take notice of something very important. It is *God's* Word, this strange word. It is what God has given (everything, his only Son) to be able to say to us. As St. Paul put it, "This was to show God's righteousness . . . , it was to prove at the present time that he himself is righteous and that he justifies him who has faith in Jesus" (Rom. 3:25). The shock of the words gets deeper. It isn't merely or even mainly that *we* needed this Word to be spoken, but that *God* wants it. It was to show his own righteousness. As the Word has it, you are just, *for Jesus' sake!* — not merely for *your* sake, for *Jesus'* sake. To put it most bluntly, what *we* think about it, whether we think we need it or not, does not matter in the first place because it is *God's* cause. God's decision is being announced. As a matter of fact, as a result of our sin, we never really want or think we need these words. But no matter, God has decided the issue; he has decided to show his own righteousness, regardless. These words are the creative words of God. Just as once God said, "Let there be light," and there was light. He didn't consult the darkness as to whether it thought it needed the light. The darkness would never admit to that. So God speaks to show his righteousness. The words are intended to do what God's Word always does, to create out of nothing, to call something new into being, to start a reformation. God, that is, has decided just to start over from scratch. So listen up!

The fact that these words fall on deaf ears is not, of course, anything new. The incident recorded in the Gospel lesson — a conversation between Jesus and some of his followers — is a clear indication of that. We are told that these were people who believed on him, so the incident is even more disturbing. "If you continue in my word," Jesus says, "you are truly my disciples, and you will know the truth, and the truth will make you free" (John 8:31-32).

"But, but, but . . . ," they said, "we aren't in bondage! We are descendents of Abraham, we're not slaves of anyone." Just as we today might say, "We are Americans, we are free people — what's this promise of freedom? Who needs it?" But the tragedy of the situation is that they didn't even know the trouble they were in. As John's Gospel often puts it, our problem is that we are in the dark, blind, even though we think we can see. So Jesus lays open the problem: "Truly, truly, everyone who commits sin is a slave of sin" (John 8:34). And a slave is in a precarious position because the days of a slave are numbered. The slave can't stay in the house forever. The slave is not an heir. The Son, however, continues forever. So if the Son really sets you free, "you will be free indeed." But then comes the worst part (left out of the lectionary — the committee always seems to leave out the worst parts): "I know that you are the children of Abraham; yet you seek to kill me, because my word finds no place in you" (8:37). There is the problem: "My word finds no place in you." The great promise of justification by faith and the freedom it brings falls on deaf ears. Indeed, so little is it wanted that the one who brings it must be killed.

Now what is the reason for all this? If we look back to the passage from Romans we find it. The reason is that we make a fundamental mistake. We think that the law is the remedy for sin. If we could just get our act together we could break the slavery and be free at last. But the Word from Romans comes like a mighty thunderbolt: "Now we know that what the law says, it speaks to those who are under the law, so that every mouth may be stopped, and the whole world may be held accountable to God" (Rom. 3:19). The law is no remedy for sin. The law can do a lot of things. It can preserve society. It can restrain evil. It can even help us to reach out to give aid beyond our normal reach. It may preserve, restrain, prevent, and so forth. Yet, it is not a remedy for sin. As a matter of fact, it just makes sin worse.

We seem to have a difficult time learning this, but it is really quite evident. To take a simple example, one might say that the law is like a stoplight. The stoplight prevents evil. It stops us from running over, or into, each other. But it doesn't stop sin — indeed it probably only makes it worse. Does it make us better people? Have you ever known anyone who likes to stop at stoplights? Don't we always try to slip through on the yellow or even that split second after it flips onto the red — hoping "John Law" isn't looking? Don't we sit growling when it doesn't change, or honk at the driver ahead who doesn't move quickly enough? And even if by some chance there were some who started a society for the preservation and veneration of stoplights, would such piety be the end of sin or only the beginning of the worst form of sin: pride? No, the law is no remedy for sin. The law shows us who we are. The law simply issues the final judgment: "For no human being will be justified in his sight by works of the law, since through the law comes knowledge of sin" (Rom. 3:20). What the law says to us is just, "No way, no exit."

So, since there is no way, since the law is no remedy for sin, God has decided to start over, to do something only God could do, to create something new — to show a righteousness completely apart from the law, sending Jesus into this world under the law, to die at our hands always so insistent on doing the law, and nevertheless to raise him up. He came saying, "Your sins are forgiven!" The response was, "Who needs it? You're wrong!" God has simply wiped out all distinctions between those who keep the law and those who don't. Isn't that crazy? But so St. Paul claims: "For there is no distinction, since all have sinned and fallen short of the glory [not the law!] of God; they are justified by his grace as a gift, through the redemption which is in Christ Jesus, whom God put forward as an expiation by his blood, to be received by faith" (Rom. 3:22-25). God has simply decided to wipe out all the distinctions and start over in Jesus. So there is simply nothing to do now but listen to the creative Word spoken into our darkness: You are just for Jesus' sake! It matters not whether you think you need it. It is the Word of God.

And if we look at it aright, this Word too is not so utterly strange. Suppose your child were to ask you, "Dad, Mom, what do I have to do to be your child?" Is there some law, some deed, some program you could propose? Perhaps the first thing you would have to do would be to weep that the question could ever be raised. But what could you say? What do you have to do to be my child? "Nothing. Just listen. Believe me. You are my child, I love you, I will never let you go." So, you see, the child is "justified by faith alone, without the deeds of law." It is, as the prophet Jeremiah wrote, a matter of a new heart — a spiritual "heart transplant," you might say. "The days are coming, says the Lord, when I will make a new covenant with my people, not like the old one, the law, which they broke again and again. I will put my law within them and write it on their

89

hearts and I will be their God and they will be my people, and they will know me, and I will forgive their iniquity and remember their sin no more" (cf. Jer. 31:31-34). It is an absolutely new start.

So today, when we think about reformation again, about something new, a new heart, a new being, a new you, I can't come to you with grand schemes and plans, or even a new set of laws, an outline for growth, a program to increase your spirituality, or — goodness knows what all. When God undertook to start over with us he didn't do anything like that. He had tried all that. Instead he sent Jesus. He decided to do something really wild, really new. He decided simply to forgive, to remember sin no more. He sent a preacher. So if these words are to come to an appropriate conclusion, there is nothing for me to do but just say it: You are just for Jesus' sake. And there is nothing for you to do but just listen. Believe it, it is for you! It will really reform your life!

# A Word from Without

*"Is not my word like fire, says the LORD, and like a hammer which breaks the rock in pieces?"*

Jer. 23:29

"Is not my word like fire, says the LORD, and like a hammer which breaks the rock in pieces?" — not exactly a user-friendly approach to the Word of the Lord. Jeremiah is not likely to be one to whom we would turn for apologetic grist for the theological mill. Indeed, it is ironic that when I was looking for a hymn that might be appropriate to this Word, I came instead upon "Your Word, O Lord, is Gentle Dew!" — well, maybe sometimes, but not today.

Jeremiah was mad. He was furious at his fellow prophets because they were filling the air with their pious dreams and blandishments, prophesying in the deceit of their own hearts, peddling their sweet nothings about God. When I read a text like this I'm constantly amazed at how contemporary it is. Things, it seems, have not changed much. In our day we have virtually banished God and his Christ from the world "out there." Religion and faith have to do with the internal world, the world "inside" the self where we coddle ourselves with our dreams: "I want my God to be gentle like the dew, and affirming and supportive and kind. . . ." So the story goes. And preachers and teachers fill the air

91

with their own opinions rather than speak a Word from the Lord. I suppose, as in Jeremiah's day, we do this because it is too fearsome to think that God is actually "out there" attending to the affairs of the world.

But Jeremiah warned that it wouldn't work. "Am I a God at hand, says the LORD, and not a god afar off?" So he thundered. "Can a man hide himself in secret places so that I cannot see him? says the LORD. Do I not fill the heaven and earth?" (vv. 23-24). We have to do with a God who comes at us from without, from out there in the world of Nebuchadrezzar, machines, things, and other people — yes, even dirt-moving caterpillars and eighteen-wheeler semis. The Word is a word from without, from outside the self and its dreams.

But now a text like this really puts us in a tight spot. Who shall presume to speak a Word from the Lord? Who can speak a Word that is from without and not just another wish-wash of pious dreams? Jeremiah made claim to do it, and of course he got into a lot of trouble. Tempting as it might be, I won't tell you my dreams, nor do I have theological opinions to peddle, even though through the years I have collected enough of them — some pretty good, if I do say so myself. Rather, I have a commission to do the fearsome business of speaking a Word from without, a Word that is like fire or like a hammer that breaks the rock in pieces.

Where shall I find such a Word? When such questions arise time and again I am taken back to what is just about my favorite passage in the *Book of Concord,* from the *Smalcald Articles* where Luther announces, "This then is the thunderbolt by means of which God with one blow destroys both open sinners and false saints. He allows no one to justify himself. . . ." And then Luther makes direct connection with Jeremiah: "*This* is the hammer of which Jeremiah speaks, 'Is not my Word like a hammer which breaks the rock in pieces?'" Talk about a Word from without! A Word that shatters both sinners and false saints with one blow! It just blows them all away. I have been around long enough to see it actually happen, to see some rejoice and some resent, to see the rocks split. What is so devastating is that when the hammer falls we, in utter bewilderment, suddenly feel we have to find something else to do.

Now I suppose I could stop here and just sit back and say, "Isn't it grand, Amen!" and have done with it. But there is one move left to make. I have to *say* it. This is no show. It is not a dry run. It is not a metaphysical dream — it's for real. A lot has happened since Jeremiah's day. Jesus has happened. The Crucified One has been raised. There is something to say, a Word from without, from beyond the grave. It is not my word or dream or opinion — that would be quite a different word, you can count on it.

So I must say it one more time since it is a matter of your eternal destiny, and it is so much fun to say: You are just for Jesus' sake, says the Lord. Now, there, is not my Word like fire, says the Lord, and like a hammer that breaks a rock in pieces?

# On Getting Out of the Way for Jesus

## John 1:6-8, 19-28

There was a man sent from God, whose name was John . . . but he was not the light. Is that not a strange and demeaning thing to say about someone — especially someone sent from God? He was not the light? Indeed, our text for today seems very concerned to tell us more what John is *not* than what he *is*. There were strange things going on down there in the wilds by the river Jordan. We have already heard about John in this Advent season in last Sunday's text from the Gospel of Mark. He appeared out of nowhere, wearing wild clothing, camel's hair held up with a strap of leather, and eating things that hardly seem appetizing, locusts and wild honey. And he cried aloud, "The time is up, Repent! Turn about! Be baptized!" Strange things indeed.

According to our text, the religious authorities in Jerusalem were getting nervous. People were flocking out to hear this wild man and to be baptized. So what did the authorities do? They did, of course, what governing authorities always do. They formed a committee to investigate the strange goings-on down by the Jordan. I suppose in our day we would call it a task force. And it would be made up of all the appropriate people and they would be charged with getting up a position paper on the troublesome business of this baptizer. So, we are told, priests and Levites were sent down from Jerusalem to get at the truth and settle the matter once and for all.

The result, you might say, was a kind of committee hearing with

94

John the Baptist in the witness stand. The committee bore in on him with its question, "Who are you?" Now, when you ask such questions you are usually expecting to get some sort of answer about what a person does, or what a person's role is. "Who are you?" "I am a business person. I am a doctor. I am a farmer. I am a professor. . . ." And so it is here. But John gives an odd answer. He says only what he is not. But it is more than just an answer; it is, we are pointedly told, a confession. He is, as it were, on the witness stand, called to make his confession. "He confessed," we are told. The writer seems to want to make sure we get it straight: "he did not deny, but confessed, 'I am not the Messiah.'"

Now the committee seems to be very frustrated at that answer, no doubt muttering to themselves, "What kind of answer is that? What did we come all this way down here from Jerusalem for, anyway? Well, if you're not the Messiah, who are you then? Are you Elijah?" It seems like a silly question to us, I suppose. But in those days there was some expectation that Elijah would return to prepare the way for the Messiah. In Matthew 17:9-13, when they come down from the Mount of Transfiguration, Jesus tells his disciples to say nothing about what had happened until the resurrection. But then, they ask, "Why do the scribes say that first Elijah must come?" Jesus responds by saying that Elijah has already come. The disciples understood him to be speaking of John the Baptist. But in our text today John flatly denies the identification: "Are you Elijah?"

"I am not," says John.

"Well then," the committee persists, "Are you the Prophet?" (Not just a prophet, but *the* Prophet.)

"No," says John, "I am not the prophet." The prophet too was an expected Messianic forerunner, someone the people longed for. In Deuteronomy 18:15 Moses promises that "The LORD your God will raise up for you a prophet like me from among you . . . him you shall heed."

"But no," says John, "I am not the prophet." You can sense the growing frustration of the committee.

"Who are you then? We have to write a report, don't you see? We need answers. Our bosses back in Jerusalem are going to be plenty mad if we don't justify our expense account, so what do you have to say for yourself?"

"Well," says John, "I am just a voice crying in the wilderness, 'Make straight the way of the Lord,' just as the prophet Isaiah said." But the committee can hardly buy that.

"That's it? Just a voice? Then what are you baptizing for? How do you explain all these people? This isn't just a voice, this is a movement!" But the answer becomes even more mysterious.

"No, it's not a movement," says John. "It all has to do with one *person*. I baptize with water, but like the baptisms of old they are only a purification rite, a preparation. There is one among you whom you do not know, and I can't even begin to touch what he will do. I'm not even worthy to untie his shoes." And there, apparently, the committee investigation ends. They had to pack up their briefcases and head back to Jerusalem. Can you imagine what their report might have been? What was this all about?

Indeed, what was it all about? Like the committee, we too are left asking the question. But, unlike the committee, we have the advantage of knowing the rest of the story. It is about advent, a coming, the coming of something absolutely new. John knew that the past was all over now, so he had to deny all direct connection with even the best hopes and dreams of the past so that he could be just a voice, so he could get out of the way for Jesus, so he could cry out, "Make straight the way of the Lord!"

What is it that is so new about this coming one? It is grace! That's what it is all about. In some of the passages left out of our assigned text we are given the key to the matter: "The Word became flesh and dwelt among us, full of grace and truth; we have beheld his glory . . . from his fulness have we all received, grace upon grace." And perhaps the key passage of all is this: "The law was given through Moses; grace and truth came through Jesus Christ" (vv. 14-17). Grace is the reason John can't begin to touch what Jesus is all about. Grace is the reason he can't even untie Jesus' shoes.

But now the problem is that grace doesn't fare so well in this world. The problem is that for many people, and in many ways, John might be made over to be a more desirable "Messiah" than Jesus. Indeed, that is no doubt the whole reason for the grilling in this text. Some interpreters think that already in those days there was a kind of sect gathering around John, claiming that he was the real Messiah. After all, who would not perhaps prefer John to Jesus? John was a tell-it-like-it-is prophet, an Elijah who could call down fire from heaven to finish off the priests of Baal, a preacher who could cry out, "You brood of vipers, who warned you to flee the wrath to come? . . . The axe is laid to the root of the trees; every tree that doesn't bear fruit will be hewn down and cast into the fire. . . . The Messiah comes with his winnowing fork in his hand. He will thresh out the wheat and throw the chaff to the winds" (Matt. 3:7-12). Or there was heroic John who stood up to Herod and got thrown in prison for his troubles and eventually had his head chopped off at the whim of a belly dancer. John the hero of justice and righteousness, who would not prefer him?

Indeed, sometimes it seems that Christians even like to turn Jesus into another John — into Jesus the great prophet who is the sublime teacher of the new law and the champion of righteousness and justice. Even preachers like to talk on and on about "prophetic ministry" and such. It might be that John himself began to wonder if Jesus was really the coming one. When he was in prison, we are told, he sent an investigating committee of his own to Jesus to ask, "Are you he who is to come or are we to look for another?" (Matt. 11:3). John might well have wondered, "Where's the axe at the root of the trees? Where's the winnowing fork? Where's the fire? Is this all there is?" But Jesus just answered, "Go and tell John what you have seen and heard: the blind see, the lame walk, lepers are cleansed, the deaf hear, the dead are raised up, and the poor have good news preached to them" — all acts of mercy, all sheer grace. But that is why our text has to warn us that, in spite of the attractiveness of John, "he was not the light." Why not? Because, of course, he brought no *grace.* In spite of all the heroics, he brought no grace. He could only bear witness to the grace. And that is the reason why he denies all the grand roles the investigating committee put up to him.

"Are you the Messiah?"

"I am not."

"Are you Elijah?"

"I am not."

"Are you the Prophet like unto Moses?"

"I am not, for what Moses brought was law, but grace and truth came through Jesus Christ!"

John the Baptist pointing the long, bony finger simply witnessed: "He must increase, I must decrease." John doesn't come to fit into the same old roles. He has no real purpose for being except to point. He is nothing. He has no role to play in this world, no real job description. All that is left is just a voice. "Who am I? I am just the voice of one crying in the wilderness, 'Make straight the way of the Lord!'"

Get ready for something absolutely new. It can't be captured in any of the old roles, it can only be a cry in this wilderness. Grace can find no place, really, among us here. Remember when some of the disciples asked Jesus where he was from? (Another one of those questions we ask to try to find out who a person is!) Jesus replied, "Foxes have holes, and the birds of the air have nests, but the Son of Man has no place to lay his head" (Matt. 8:20). Just as there was no room for him in the inn, there is not much room for grace. Indeed, it was because he came to bring the grace of forgiveness that he was eventually crucified. John was killed because he preached the law to Herod. Jesus was killed because he preached grace. So there is no room here. There is just a voice crying in the wilderness.

And so today, just as way back then, you too, my friends, are left with only a voice. And I, for better or for worse, must speak it once again: "Make straight the way of the Lord." What is coming? Grace! Forgiveness, the true light of the world! Not more law — *grace*. The law was given by Moses, but that is all over now. Grace and truth come through Jesus Christ. And it is for you! Why must we make the way straight? Because, no doubt, this is the real test. Can we bear the grace of God? John was right, you know, the axe *is* laid to the root of the trees, and you can hear the swoosh of the winnowing fork. But it turns out not to be law that is the real test, but grace! For this was the judgment, says Jesus, that they believed not in me. But God in his infinite love, mercy, and patience has granted us yet another chance to hear the voice. The Word was made flesh and dwelt among us and we beheld his glory, full of grace and truth . . . and of his fullness we have all received, grace for grace. Believe it! It is for you! It will save you!

# The Perilous Journey

*"He left the ninety and nine in the wilderness and went to seek the one that was lost."*

from Luke 15:1-7

He left the ninety and nine in the wilderness and went to seek the one that was lost. A perilous, perilous journey. Who can fathom it? Can it ever succeed? The odds are not good: ninety-nine to one! Why so perilous? Because it is a great offense to go after just one. It is an offense first of all to the ninety-nine. What are they to think, after all, left there in the lurch in the wilderness, deserted by a seemingly sentimental shepherd who goes after the one — just one? If he had left them safe in the fold maybe it wouldn't have been so bad. But in the wilderness? What was he thinking? Doesn't he know that religion is a matter of community? Doesn't he give heed to statistics, or to the law of averages or cost-efficiency? What is the majority (moral or immoral) supposed to think? Why should the ninety-nine bother to stay in line if the shepherd is going to lavish all this attention on one mangy stray? Or what is one to think at a place like this, a seminary of higher learning, where universals are stock in trade and where what "always" happens is carefully observed and codified? Is not such a shepherd a little embarrassing? Above all, how can this be a parable of the mercy of God? Doesn't God love everybody? The whole affair, you see, is a mighty offense to the ninety and nine. After all, who ever heard of such a journey? Is it not supposed to be that the ninety-nine seek the shepherd?

Perilous journey, to go after the one who is lost. Can it ever succeed? There seem to be sets of formidable roadblocks, a kind of conspiracy of silence (not to say blindness and stone-deafness) that makes it impossible to see or hear what this journey is really about. The tragedy of the ninety-nine, it seems, was that they just didn't get it. They murmured, the text says, and complained. Is it not dangerous to receive sinners and eat with them? How can one just up and forgive here in this place? Who can claim such authority? Won't folks get the wrong idea? Isn't it all too cheap? Isn't the time of the need for forgiveness long gone? How can one run a world in which the shepherd leaves the ninety-nine and goes after the one who is lost?

Well, the ultimate tragedy is that one can't. At least not in this world. He can't get by with it. But this crazy shepherd has a one-track mind. He just keeps to his journey. And in the end, they — we — get him for it. Did him in, we did. Put him on a cross. But he stayed with it. He said, "Father, forgive them, for they know not what they do." Perilous journey — to seek the one that is lost!

But if there is peril in leaving the ninety-nine in their scandalized bitterness, perhaps that is not even half the battle. For what of the one upon whom all this attention is lavished? Are there not endless possibilities for offense there too? It could be, could it not, that the one doesn't even know or care that it is lost? Maybe it left the fold because they were, after all, a rather boring lot with their safety-first piety. Suppose that when the shepherd comes struggling through the wilderness the little lost lamb just bleats, "What are you doing way out here, Mr. Shepherd? You are wasting your time. I'm not lost, I'm just worshipping God in nature," or as theologians like to say, "I'm just into first-article concerns!" Or it could be, could it not, that the one who is lost might be offended by becoming the object of so much religious attention: "Why pick on me?" the lost one might well ask, "am I the only one?" There is a mighty offense here as well. The one could just be spooked into running away and hiding all the more!

So it was not strange that in the end it was one of his own who betrayed him. Why? I expect it has something to do with the fact that he got just too close and the one took offense and betrayed him into the hands of the many.

Perilous journey, to go after the one who is lost! But he stops at nothing. He leaves all — including abstractions, generalizations, universals — behind, no matter how much we stall, filibuster, or betray. He dies to all that. But even that won't stop him. He comes back, even from the dead, to say, "Peace."

So where are we today? What does it all add up to? If we have listened aright we will realize — as is always the case with the parables of Jesus — that we too are caught in the web the parable weaves. If we have listened aright we will begin to see that this is the last leg of the journey, this meeting today, here and now — the last and perhaps the most perilous leg of all, one last chasm to cross. For there is one final thing this shepherd enjoins me to say. It was, it is, for you. You are the one, now that you hear my voice. Is that not preposterous, wild, and scandalous? But what else can it be? Where do you find your place in this story? "There is more joy in heaven," we are told, "over one sinner who repents than over ninety-nine who need no repentance." Ah, but are there such who need no repentance? Is this perhaps our last escape hatch? Are we not already good Christians? What would that mean? That this whole, arduous, perilous journey has ended at the wrong address? Would that not be the most monstrous misadventure of all?

Well, I expect you shall have to answer that question for yourselves. For my part, I can only say that I have been invited to preach here today. So preach I shall. There is nothing for me to do, then, but to fling those words across the last chasm. It is for you. You are the one. You see, this man has an odd taste in friends. This man receives sinners and eats with them. Thanks be to God!

# Go Away, Jesus!

*What have you to do with us, O Son of God? Have you come here to torment us before the time?*

from Matt. 8:28-34

What shall we do with Jesus? A Jesus who carries on in such outrageous fashion? Or what shall I do, faced with the prospect of having to preach on such a preposterous text? Shall I seek, somehow, to make sense of it for you, to apologize for this Jesus so you can sit back and assume that all is well after all? In this regard it is almost comical to watch the various commentators stumbling over themselves to defend Jesus. What lies nearest to hand, perhaps, is to moralize somehow, like "they hadn't ought to have been raising pigs anyway." The pig, the *Jerome Bible Commentary* sets forth for our edification, is the most unclean animal. A pig was good for nothing at all and no one could incur a loss when a herd of pigs perished. I wonder how that would go down in Iowa? One commentator even suggested that the owner could, after all, have cut his losses by making hams out of the drowned pigs (the original deviled ham, perhaps?). Was he serious? Or one might perhaps psychologize: we have to do here only with primitive perceptions of mental illness, of course, even though the text doesn't have all that much to do with us. Another commentator suggests that what happened, perhaps, was that the shrieking and carrying on of the alleged demoniacs frightened this herd of swine grazing nearby so that they stampeded into the sea and this was taken as a sign of comfort — an indication that they really had been cured! Ah yes! So we can all relax! But yet one can still hear, nevertheless, the protest of those poor herdsmen: "But I don't care about all that religious claptrap. I lost my hawgs, don't you see?" Better a few crazies hanging around now and then than that! The verdict of the townspeople when they came out to see the wild goings-on is not strange either, I think: "When they saw him, they begged him to leave their neighborhood." You see, it didn't really matter, after all, whether they were supposedly crazy or sane, whether apology was possible or not, whether the reaction was rage, fright, or even awe. The outcome was the same: "Go away, Jesus! What have you to do with us? Have you come to torment us before the time?"

What *shall* we do with Jesus? Could it be, perhaps, could it just be, that the matter is quite other than we think? Could it be that this Jesus is waging a lonely and desperate battle for us all by himself of dimensions so deep and mysterious we can only dimly perceive them with elemental spirits and principalities and powers? Could it be that with infinite patience he waits for us to see? Could it be that when one looks into the depths of a text like this the greatest miracle is that he doesn't just let us go, leave us among the tombs with the demons, send us cascading into the sea, or even just blow it all away? What was it he said once? Only the one who loses his very life for my sake shall find it? Could it be, after all, that the only real comfort we might offer those herdsmen — for the time being, at least — is, "Count your blessings. You may be lucky that you lost only your hogs"?

That, however, may be too much for us to contemplate. Safer it is, no doubt, to stay with the plea, "Go away, Jesus. What have you to do with us? Have you come here to torment us before the time?" But then, we are left, of course, with the disturbing question of those demons. Where have they gone? Were they drowned in the sea? Did they fall into some psychotherapeutic slough? Legend has it that they like the sea, that it is one of their favorite haunts. Where could they have gone — if it is not yet time? Well, where better to look than in a world which in a myriad of ways — subtle and not so subtle — still mouths the same plea: "Go away, Jesus"? Where better to look, perhaps, than in a church which still finds it so necessary, apparently, to apologize for the strange goings-on in the country of the Gadarenes? Where better to look than in that zoo which calls itself "Evangelical Christianity"? Where better to look, even, than in the mirror — perhaps the mirror of a text like this?

For isn't it strange — and marvelous — that somehow the more we plead with him to go away, the more surely he moves in upon us? The more we try to get rid of him, the more tightly he closes in with majestic constancy? We tried to get rid of him once and for all by nailing him to a cross. But that only means we can't ever get rid of him or be finished with him. We sealed him in a tomb, but the stone was rolled away and he came back to say, "Shalom." "Peace be unto you." He even said, "It is expedient for you that I go away, for I will send you another comforter. I will never leave you" (cf. John 16:7; 14:16-18).

So the last question: "Is it still before the time?" Or might it be that the time is up now? What shall we do with Jesus? What is left to do but repent? For he comes to save us from our sins and to cast out the demons. What is left but to begin to stammer, somehow, *Maranatha,* come Lord Jesus.

# I Chose You

## John 15:9-17

"You did not choose me, but I chose you." Imperious words! Disconcerting words, perhaps even shocking words — especially amid all this rather nice talk in John's Gospel about love and friendship and joy. Everything seems to be going along swimmingly and smoothly in this discourse about the vine and the branches: "As the Father has loved me, so I have loved you; abide in my love." That is certainly nice, isn't it?

"If you keep my commandments, you will abide in my love." Now that may be a little strenuous, but it sounds fair enough, I guess — the kind of thing one would expect, after all, from a preacher or a religious leader. After all, we have to do something, you know.

"These things I have spoken to you that my joy may be in you, and that your joy may be full." Now *that* I can really resonate to — joy! I'm for that!

"This is my commandment, that you love one another." Just think, all we have to do is love one another. We can really run with that too, I expect, just like some prototypical contextual ethicist.

And not only that: "You are my friends if you do what I command you. No longer do I call you servants . . . but I have called you friends. . . ." Just think, no heavy agenda here, just friends of Jesus. What a friend we have in Jesus! Isn't that nice? Everything is reasonably under control so far.

But then Jesus says this: "You did not choose me, but I chose you."

Like a bolt from the blue, a comet from some strange and unknown realm. Now what did Jesus have to go and say that for? Just when we were getting on so nicely! What are such words doing here? Could anything be more calculated to break up our cozy little friendship than that? I mean, it's alright for him to love us, of course, but does he have to go and say he chooses us? What shall we do with such disturbing words? Shall we just pass over them in silence — as we are most likely to do — and try to go on as though nothing has happened?

Or could it possibly be that those imperious words are really the key, indeed, the climax, to this whole discourse about the vine and the branches? Could it be that here everything we had so comfortably presupposed about the cozy relationship is simply turned on its head? That *he* is *really* the vine, the source, the sustenance, the life-giver, and that we are just branches, after all? And could it be that that is exactly the point? Could it be that the organic image translated into human and relational terms simply means, "You did not choose me, but I chose you"?

Suddenly even the cozy relationship of friendship usually assumed among us is set on its ear. For us friendship is neutral, reciprocal, and a compact of equal exchange. But it is not the case that we sought his friendship, and certainly not that there was any basis within us on which we could do so; it is not, apparently, what a friend *we* have in Jesus, but simply that *he* has decided. How could we cope with that if it were not for the "as I have loved you"? And how could we take him at his word, "You are my friends if you do what I command you," if it were not for the fact that he has simply decided to call us his friends, and laid down his life for those very friends?

"No, you did not choose me," Jesus says, "but that sorry chapter is now closed. It's over for good. We need not argue about that. But now there is a new future. For I have chosen you and appointed you that you should bear fruit and that your fruit should last — last forever, indeed, so that whatever you ask the Father *in my name,* he may give it to you." This "I," I the one who chose you in spite of everything, I your Lord, commands you to love one another. And that will last.

You did not choose me but I chose you. Imperious words indeed. But it is the gospel truth. And now, since we meet once again to partake

of the Lord's last supper with his chosen ones, we cannot do that without noting that these words in John's Gospel are Jesus' farewell to his
own. They stand in John's Gospel just in that place where the supper
stands. They are, you might say, in an intimate sense, something of the
same thing. You did not choose me, but I chose you. "This is my body
given for you, this is my blood shed for you for the forgiveness of sins.
When you eat the bread and drink the cup, hear the words: 'I am the
vine, you are the branches . . . without me you can do nothing.'" And of
course hear these words at the same time: "You did not choose me, but I
chose you and appointed you that you should bear fruit, and that your
fruit should last; abide in my love, and know that it is for you."

## On Death to Self

Matt. 17:22-27 and 26:47-56

We speak a good deal during Lent about that supreme mystery of our faith, the death to self. For, as we have heard, he who would save his life shall lose it, and he who loses his life for Jesus' sake shall find it. But what does that really mean — to die to self? Does it mean, perhaps, selling my car and going on foot or by bus? It might. We can't rule out the possibility. Does it mean, perhaps, selling my good clothes and furniture so that my wife and I should sit around in rags on orange crates? It might. Certainly we can't dismiss that possibility either. For the problem is that unless words like "dying to self" are translated into some kind of action, or something that actually happens — that is, some real change — they don't have any real meaning. So we certainly must try, eventually, to translate them into the language of action.

But before we get too hasty and impatient there are some things at which we should take a hard look. The first is that we have a rather incurable tendency always to refuse to really listen to the words of God and instead to translate them immediately into something *we* are going to do, indeed, *can* do. This is what we always do with the law. We take it and translate it into a do-it-yourself kit for salvation. It is as though we think we are going to do God a big favor by living up to what is demanded of us and even, possibly, put him out of the salvation business by accomplishing all or at least some of it ourselves — even if that turns out to be just a teeny-weeny little bit. But when we do that we really come a-cropper when we come to this word about dying to self. For what can that possibly mean in a do-it-yourself religion? Here God has set a snare for us in our easy confidence that we are big enough to handle the job. For this is a word that we find difficult to handle. We find ourselves forced either to ignore it — which we mostly do — or to try to cut it down to size so we can handle it — maybe by selling our car or our furniture or our clothes. But even then we can't rest too easily with it, for we are never quite sure that that is enough. For however much discomfort such actions may cause us, is that really dying to self? They may be just another means of keeping myself in the business of doing God big — or little — favors, and thus of protecting myself from really hearing the words. The trouble is that the self keeps getting in the way.

But what then does it really mean? When considering this question, I was struck by some of the incidents recorded in our texts for today. For here we have the picture of Jesus on the way to *his* death. His disciples are with him, and are apparently figuring that they are going to have a hand in what is about to happen. They want to go along. They want to help out, to do their bit in the business of bringing in God's kingdom, even, as Peter says in Mark's account, if that means sacrificing their lives. But the really difficult thing for them to take, as I suspect it also is for us as "religious" people, is that in the final analysis there is absolutely and utterly nothing they can do. When Jesus sets his face to go to Jerusalem, Peter wants to do something about it. He sets himself in the way and says, "God forbid, Lord! Don't do it! Don't go!" Peter wants to do God a favor — to protect and preserve the Messiah and his kingdom. But Jesus looks at him and says, "Get thee behind me Satan! For you are hindrance to me, you are not on the side of God, but of men" (Mark 8:33). This, Jesus says, is something that must happen; it is going to happen because God wants it, and there is absolutely nothing you can do about it.

And at the betrayal in the Garden of Gethsemane when the crowd comes out against Jesus with swords and clubs, they still want to do something. They still want to do their bit for God. They want to take up the sword and risk their lives, perhaps, and fight. One of them grasps a sword and cuts off the ear of one of the assailants. But Jesus will have none of it: "Put up your sword," he says, "for there is absolutely nothing you can do!" In Luke's account, Jesus even stretches out his hand to *undo* what the disciples had tried to do — he heals the wounded man. At that point, no doubt, everything within us cries out in protest along with the disciples. Is there nothing we can do? Could we not at least perhaps stage a protest march on God's behalf? Could we not seek, perhaps, an interview with Pilate? Could we not try to influence the "power structures"? Something — however small? But the unrelenting answer comes back, "No, there is nothing you can do, absolutely nothing. If there were something to be done, my Father would send legions of angels to fight!" But there is nothing to be done. "For how then should the Scriptures be fulfilled, that it *must* be so?" And when it finally came to that last and bitter moment, when these good religious men finally realized that there was nothing they could do, they forsook him and fled.

Can you see it? Can you see that hidden in these very words, these very events, is that death itself which you fear so much coming to meet you? For there is nothing that the old man — the self which must die — fears so much as having *everything* taken out of his hands. When they finally saw there was nothing they could do they forsook him and fled before the awesome truth. You, who presume to do business with God, can you see it? Can you see that this death of self is not, in the final analysis, something you can do? For the point is that God has once and for all reserved for himself the business of your salvation. There is nothing you can do now but, as the words of the old hymn have it, "climb Calvary's mournful mountain" and stand with your helpless arms at your side and tremble before "that miracle of time, God's own sacrifice complete! It is finished; hear him cry; learn of Jesus Christ to die!"

Can you see it? Can you see that really the last, bitter death is there? That in that cross God has stormed the last bastion of the self, the last presumption that you really were going to do something for him? Can you see that the death of Jesus Christ *is* your death? He has died *in your place!* He has done it. He made it. He created a salvation in the midst of time and his enemies. He is God happening to you. It is all over, finished, between you and God! He died in your place that death which you must die; he has done it in such a way as to *save* you. He has borne the whole thing! The fact that there is nothing left for you to do *is* the death of self and new birth of the new creature. He died to make a new creature of you, and as he arose, to raise you up to trust God alone.

If you can see it, perhaps then you can see, or perhaps at least begin to see, what is the *power* of God's grace and rejoice. For that is the other side of the coin once you have gotten out of your self-enclosed system. Then perhaps you can turn away from yourself, maybe really for the first time, and look upon your neighbors. Maybe for the first time you can begin to receive creation as a gift, a sheer gift from God's hands. And who knows what might happen in the power of this grace? All possibilities are open. You might sell your car, or even give it away — for someone else. You might find even that you could swallow your pride and stage a protest march — for your neighbor — or begin to seek to influence the power structures! For in the power of his cross the way is open! The way is open to begin, at least, perhaps in faltering ways, in countless little ways, to realize what it means to die to self. For that, in the final analysis, is his gift to you, the free gift of the new man, the new woman, the one who can live in faith and hope, for whom all possibilities are open!

# We Are Being Transformed

## Rom. 12:1-3

"Do not be conformed to this world but be transformed by the renewal of your mind, that you may prove what is the will of God, what is good and acceptable and perfect."

I am not at all sure that I like that text. That may come as no surprise to many of you, perhaps especially those of you who keep nipping at my heels to get me to say something about the Christian life, change, progress, and the like. But what bothers me about the text is not, I expect, what you might think. If it were simply a matter of change, or of making some sort of progress toward what we might call perfection or whatever, I reckon I could manage that as well as the next person. Like Paul, I don't want to boast, but if you want to argue on that human level I don't know that I am doing so badly! I come from three generations of pastors, have one wife, pay my dues and taxes, try to take care of my kids, go to church, work hard, keep publishing, stay out of debt, remain under the law — blameless, one could say (sort of, anyway!). No, that's not what bothers me about such a text. All that would be, when all is said and done, merely a kind of conformity to the fashions and fads of the age.

What bothers me about this text is the syntax, the grammar, and above all, the context. What bothers me is that it is put in the passive voice: not "transform your life" but "be transformed by the renewal of your mind." I think I could cope with an exhortation to get with it and transform. But what to do with an exhortation to *be transformed* — by the renewal of the mind, yet! What could that possibly mean? Well, there is the matter of the context: "Now then," Paul says, "if you have been gotten at by the mercies of God, present your bodies as a living sacrifice." Lay your bodies on the line! How so? Why this *therefore,* this "now then," as we might put it, this "now that you have gotten it straight from the shoulder"?

Above all what bothers me is that Paul has just completed his probe into the greatest mystery of them all, the mystery which tore his very soul in two to its ultimate depths, the question of election and/or rejection. The most difficult thing of all to cope with was the fact that it seemed as though those who strove with might and main to attain righteousness were cut off. They did not attain; yet those who did not strive at all attained! It is the absolute, shocking fact that those who were obedient were apparently shot down while those who were disobedient were welcomed. Not, of course, that disobedience is any accomplishment or qualification for anything, but simply that the one who stands above us all, the divine potter, calls the shots and so desires to have it so. God, the electing one, Paul says, simply shut up all things under disobedience that he might have mercy on all. "O the depth of the riches and wisdom and knowledge of God! How unsearchable are his judgments and how inscrutable his ways! For who has known the mind of the Lord, or who has been his counselor? Or who has given a gift to him that he might be repaid? For from him and through him and to him are all things. To him be glory forever. Amen" (Rom. 11:33-36).

What does it all add up to? Transformation is God's business. That's the point. Let the utterly shocking fact that God shut up all things under disobedience in order that he might have mercy on all just seep down into the depths of your soul, and wise up! That radical divine interruption in our chosen paths and cherished personal agendas, whether we are disobedient or obedient, is the only thing that is going to do any transforming to the likes of us, inveterate conformists that we are. Precisely those things we resist so desperately and kick and fuss about, that unconditional grace, that justification by faith alone, precisely those things are the transforming moves of God. If we are transformed at all, we are transformed by that. It is indeed profoundly upset-ting. You could bust a gut, burn yourself out, like Paul on the Damascus road, following what seems to you to be some urgent divine imperative. But God could just blow it all into a cocked hat. But you should know that. God is in the transformation business: "*be* transformed by the re-newal of your mind, that you may prove what is the *will of God.*" That's it, you see, the *will of God.* He will have his way with us at the last.

And what does that mean for us? It means a whole lot of things. Paul has a long list of them in the verses and chapters that follow which you can look at if you are curious: Let love be genuine; bless those who per-secute you; live in harmony; repay no one evil for evil; feed your enemy; overcome evil with good; even be subject to the higher powers — any one of which is enough to occupy a lifetime, I would guess. Here and now we have time for just one thing, the one which heads the whole list: "By the grace given to me," Paul says, "I bid everyone among you not to think of yourself more highly than you ought, but to think with sober judgment" (Rom. 12:3). Interesting that that should come first. No doubt it is the first step in that "renewal of the mind." And with good reason. For one of the greatest problems in talking about the Christian life is the high inflation rate. We blather easily about progress and change and growing or growing old gracefully and becoming more saintly and so on and so forth. The enterprise easily becomes something like a gigantic balloon that rises only by virtue of its own hot air until perchance it goes too high and comes crashing ignominiously to earth. "Think with sober judgment," Paul says. Is it not rather the case that the older you grow, the harder it gets in many ways? It takes a lot of grace to fight the battle with age and death. You get more set and crotchety, self-protective and so on, and it gets harder to keep from getting cynical and angry or from feeling cheated by life or feeling that you "blew it." "Will Grandma and Grandpa go to heaven?" a young child asks. "I hope so," says the Mother, "why do you ask?" "Well," comes the reply, "they never want to go anyplace." Yes, that's the trouble. Maybe it looks from the outside as though we sin less, but that is probably only because we are tired! We shouldn't mistake encroaching senility for sanctification.

Let no one think of herself more highly than she ought. Yes, that is the trick. For starters at least. And I suppose something like that is precisely the transformation, to be stripped of our illusions, to gain something of what Camus would call *lucidity* about who we are and what we are up to. For what do we have in the end but that shocking mercy which makes God God, and us human? The realization that in the end we shall have to be saved by grace alone? What do we have other than that promise, as Paul could put it in 2 Corinthians 3, that we all, with unveiled face beholding the glory of the Lord, *are being changed,* into his likeness from one degree of glory to another. All the high-sounding rhetoric is like a veil which covers the truth. Moses' face was veiled so that you could not see that the splendor was really fading, that Moses was dying like the rest of us. But with all the illusion gone in unveiled faces beholding the glory of the Lord — that's what does it, the shock of that grace — *we are being changed* from one degree of glory to another. Let us believe that. That we may taste what is the will of God, what is good and acceptable and perfect.

# What Matters

*But far be it from me to glory except in the cross of our Lord Jesus Christ, by which the world has been crucified to me and I to the world. For neither circumcision counts for anything, nor uncircumcision, but a new creation. Peace and mercy be upon all who walk by this rule, upon the Israel of God.*

Gal. 6:14-16

What matters? Neither circumcision nor uncircumcision matters at all, but a new creation. End of story. The last word. The parting shot. At least, so Paul winds up his epistle to the Galatians. And I thought that undoubtedly rather belligerent proclamation might be a good word for this Reformation Day, which, we should not fail to take notice, also falls during the 450th anniversary of the year of the death of Martin Luther. And it is well for us, I trust, to hear once again some of Luther's words on the matter from his 1535 lectures on Galatians:

> It is amazing that Paul should say that in Christ Jesus neither circumcision nor uncircumcision counts for anything. He should rather have said: "Either circumcision or uncircumcision counts for something, since these two are contrary to each other." But now he denies that either one counts, as though he were saying: "We must go higher, for

circumcision and uncircumcision are far too low to count for righteousness in the sight of God. They are, of course, contrary to each other, but that has nothing to do with Christian righteousness, which is not earthly but heavenly and therefore does not consist in physical things. And so whether you receive circumcision or do not receive it is all the same, for neither counts for anything in Christ Jesus."

Now I suppose few if any of us here lose much sleep today over the question of circumcision or uncircumcision. It is not likely to turn up on the scale of family values that our politicians crow about. Indeed, not only does the issue of one versus the other not matter at all to us, but the whole question itself seems strangely parochial and of no real concern.

But let us stop and ponder the matter a bit. The fact that the question doesn't matter to us is likely to mean, in the first place, of course, that we don't take the Old Testament very seriously. Or even further, if the question itself is of no concern for us, then is it not likely that the great promise of this text, that which really matters — the new creation — will be of little concern as well? For surely the only thing that displaces circumcision is not anything so pedestrian as unconcern, but the new creation. Make no mistake, without the new creation what is there but circumcision or uncircumcision?

Frankly, the aim of this parting shot in Paul's epistle is to put an end to the matter of what really matters once and for all. Nothing matters now but the new creation, *nothing!* All avenues, all escape routes are closed. Luther put it nicely: "With the two terms 'circumcision' and 'uncircumcision' Paul excludes everything that belongs to the whole universe and denies that it counts for anything in Christ Jesus." The God of all grace and mercy whose intention it is to relate to us through faith and trust has (you might say) two big problems with us — both of which destroy the relationship God purposes.

One is quite obvious. It is the problem designated by "uncircumcision," or the problem of our lawlessness, our existence among the lesser breeds without the law, our immorality and waywardness and heedlessness, even our temptation to boast in it. We are all aware enough of such things to acknowledge the problem and to recognize that it destroys faith and trust.

But the other problem is more subtle, and mostly hidden from us, especially at this place. It is really the main one that Paul wrestles with in his letters. It is the problem of the "circumcision," the problem of our lawfulness, our morality, our holiness, our so-called sanctification, our do-it-yourself religions, and all of that. What we don't see is that the "circumcision" destroys the relationship of faith and trust as surely as the "uncircumcision."

So now God has acted finally in this very proclamation by his apostle to have his way with us. God has taken the whole business out of our hands. Neither your lawlessness nor your lawfulness, your immorality nor your morality, your unholiness nor your holiness — none of it matters a bit now, but a new creation. Indeed, in most radical fashion, Paul announces not only that it no longer matters but that it is now exposed as sin! "The scripture consigned all things — good and bad! — to sin, that what was promised to faith in Jesus Christ might be given to those who believe." "Whatever is not of faith is sin" (Gal. 3:22; Rom. 14:23). All escape routes shut down. There is nothing to be done now but just listen. Neither circumcision nor uncircumcision counts for anything, but a new creation. Peace and mercy be upon all who walk by this rule.

54139041R00077

Made in the USA
Lexington, KY
03 August 2016